Games

for
Infants

Second edition

Jim Hall

A & C Black • London

D0997785

046501

LEAPFROGS

465012
372.86044
Growers
£9

- 6 DEC 2005

First published 1996 by
A & C Black Publishers Ltd
37 Soho Square, London W1D 3QZ

Second edition 2003
First edition 1996

© 2003, 1996 Jim Hall

ISBN 0 7136 6673 0

All rights reserved. No part of this publication may be reproduced in
any form or by any means – graphic, electronic or mechanical,
including photocopying, recording, taping or information storage and
retrieval systems – without the prior permission in writing of the publishers.

Jim Hall has asserted his right under the Copyright, Designs and
Patents Act, 1988, to be identified as the author of this work.

A CIP catalogue record for this book
is available from the British Library.

Note Whilst every effort has been made to ensure that the content of
this book is as technically accurate as possible, neither the author
nor the publishers can accept responsibility for any injury or loss
sustained as a result of the use of this material.

Cover illustration by Eleanor King
Cover design by James Watson

A & C Black use paper produced with elemental chlorine-free pulp,
harvested from managed sustainable forests.

Printed and bound in Great Britain by Bookcraft, Bath.

Contents

Key Stage 1: the main features

'The government believes that two hours of physical activity a week, including the National Curriculum for physical education and extra-curricular activities, should be an aspiration for all schools. This applies to all key stages.'

Programme of Study

Pupils should be taught to:

a travel with, send and receive a ball and other equipment in different ways. Equipment used in the following lessons includes balls of various sizes and textures, bats, rackets, bean bags, quoits, skipping ropes of different lengths, and hoops.

b develop these skills for simple net, striking/fielding and invasion-type games. Neat, controlled footwork with changes of speed and direction used to pursue, dodge or simply to give you ample practising room, makes chasing games more exciting and safe, and develops a more caring attitude towards self and others.

c play simple, competitive net, striking/fielding and invasion-type games that they and others have made, using simple tactics for attacking and defending. From the simplest 'Can you aim at the line between you and your partner and count your good hits to see who is the winner?' to 'Can you invent a simple, 1 against 1 game, using one ball and a part of a line, and using the skill we have just practised?' to 'Can your group of four make up a game, using the large ball and two of the lines round the area?'.

At every stage the pupils will be asked to consider 'How will you score in your little game? What will be the main rule to make the game fair for everyone? How will your game re-start after a score? Can you think of any extra ways to score to make the game more exciting?', and, if necessary, 'How can we help to make scoring easier?' (e.g. defending team will be 'passive', not going for the ball).

Attainment Target:

Pupils should be able to demonstrate that they can:

a select and use skills, actions and ideas appropriately, applying them with co-ordination and control (e.g. throw ball up, jump to catch it, land nicely poised).

b vary, copy, repeat and link skills, actions and ideas in ways that suit the activities (i.e. ample equipment needed to provide an implement each to enable such practising).

c talk about differences between own and others' work; suggest improvements; and use this understanding to improve their own performance (questioning following a demonstration requires a more detailed answer than 'It was nice').

d recognise and describe the changes that happen to the body during exercise (from increased warmth, perspiration, deeper breathing, chest rising and falling, and fatigue, to 'feeling relaxed, calm, happy, good inside, proud, excited').

Main NC Headings when considering progression and expectation

- **Planning** – in a safe, thoughtful, focused way, thinking ahead to an intended outcome. The set criteria are used and there is evidence of originality and variety.

- **Performing and improving performance** – pupils work hard, concentrating on the main feature of the task, to present a neat, efficient, poised and confident performance, totally under control.

- **Linking actions** – pupils work hard, concentrating on the main features of the task, to present a neat, poised and confident performance, totally under control.

- **Reflecting and making judgements** – pupils describe what they and others have done; tell what they like about a performance; give an opinion on how it might be improved; and then can be seen and copied because we remember what we see.

Playground games equipment

- Sets of 30 of: small balls; medium balls; large balls; bean bags; skipping ropes; playbats; hoops; short tennis rackets.
- 10 x long 24ft (7m) skipping ropes for group skipping and as 'nets' for tennis and quoits.
- 10 x rubber quoits. • 6 x 8in (20cm) foam balls.
- Playground chalk. • 1 x set Kwik Cricket.
- 8 x marker cones.

The playground games 'classroom'

Infant school Games lessons should be taught out of doors on the playground. Where no netball court is marked, the 'classroom' is a painted rectangle, of six to eight 8-10 metre square grids.

The painted rectangle is essential because it:

a contains the class in a limited space within which the teacher can see, manage and be easily heard by the whole class

b gives the spaces needed for the three activities of the final group practices part of the lesson. Each space is normally two adjacent rectangles across the court. Where there are eight grids or small rectangles, two pairs can be used for any activity that benefits from extra space, such as short tennis

c prevents accidents by keeping the class well away from any potential hazards such as concrete seats, hutted classrooms, fences or walls, all of which should be several metres outside the games rectangle

d provides lines which are used in hundreds of ways during the infant years programme. Pupils run and jump over; balance on; can be 'safe' on in chasing games; aim at; play net games over; use in limited area 'invent a game or practice' situations; play end to end, two with or two against games; do side-to-side sprint relays.

Teaching playground games

1 Essential traditions include the safe, unselfish sharing of space; immediate responses to instructions, particularly the one to 'Stop!'; and a quiet atmosphere with pupils keen to improve. The class should understand they must be 'found working, not waiting' as their contribution to almost non-stop activity.

2 Inaction and 'lesson dead spots' are caused by over-long explanations; too many stoppages for demonstrations followed by lengthy comments and discussion; and poor responses from a class who need to be asked to 'Stop!' far too often.

3 Most of the teaching will be from just outside the rectangle, looking in, so that no-one is behind the teacher's back.

4 While the thinking and planning, reflecting and evaluating requirements of the NC should always be a concern, henceforth, in teaching PE, the main emphasis must always be on the doing, the performing, the action.

5 The teacher's aim should be a flowing, almost non-stop lesson with optimum activity. Children enjoy a lesson when 'it is fun; is exciting; has lots of action; all have a turn; you learn interesting new things; it makes you fitter; rules make it fair for everyone.'

Lesson Plan – 30 minutes

Emphasis on: (a) creating a quiet, industrious atmosphere with quick responses; (b) sharing the space sensibly and safely with others; (c) practising to learn, improve and remember the skills being taught.

WARM-UP AND FOOTWORK PRACTICES - 4 minutes

1 Show me your best running as you go to all parts of our playground 'classroom'. Visit the ends, the sides, the middle and always keep inside the lines of our pretend classroom.

2 Good running is quiet, and you do not follow anyone.

3 When I call 'Stop!', can you be in a big space, all by yourself?

4 Now run and jump over the lines. When I call 'Stop!' next time, can you run to balance, tall and still, on a line?

SKILL PRACTICES: WITH BEAN BAGS - 10 minutes

Individual practices

1 Can you throw up with one hand and catch with two hands? Throw your bean bag up to about head height.

2 Now, can you walk, throwing up with two hands and catching with two hands? Watch the bean bag carefully all the time.

3 Aim to land the bean bag on a line or mark on the ground. Pick it up, then aim carefully at another line. Swing your throwing arm forward and back, then aim and throw.

Partner practices

1 Can you walk, side by side, handing the bean bag to your partner?

2 Stand, facing your partner and make gentle, little throws to each other. Aim for your partner's outstretched hands.

3 Now can you show me a way in which you and your partner can throw or send the bean bag to each other? (For example, walking, side by side, small throws; place bag on top of shoe, kick it to partner; aim to land it on partner's flat hands; walk, balancing it on the back of a hand, slide sideways on to partner's flat hand.)

GROUP PRACTICES - 16 minutes

1 Hoop each. Practise freely, sometimes with the hoop on the ground, sometimes holding or sending it. (For example, balancing on ground; hold, throw, catch; send by bowling.)

2 Bean bag with a partner. Have three turns each, aiming at the hoop on the ground, then change over. Swing a long, slow arm. Aim high enough for bean bag to 'see' and fly into the hoop.

3 Medium size ball each. Show me how you can send the ball a little distance, up in the air or to other parts of this group's space (For example, kick, roll, head, bounce, throw, bat.)

Lesson Notes • 4 Lessons Development

WARM-UP AND FOOTWORK PRACTICES

1 The emphasis is on running within the confines of the outside four lines of the area. Regular stopping of the running to bring wayward children back 'inside the lines, please' starts the development of this important tradition. Inside the lines is contained; they can hear the teacher; and they are well clear of dangerous fences, huts, concrete benches, etc.

2 A demonstration by a silent runner, moving lightly with heels and knees uplifted, explains 'quiet running'.

3 Not being near others can be practised by a sudden 'Stop!' by the teacher which should show them not near others, all facing different ways, and not in an anti-clockwise circle, common in infant schools running.

4 Running and jumping over lines alternates with a held balance, 'tall and still' on tiptoes on the nearest line, when the teacher calls 'Stop!' (Responding to the signal 'Stop!' immediately is being practised often with this new class to establish an essential standard of listening and responding.)

SKILLS PRACTICES

Individual practices

1 A teacher demonstration of the one-handed throw to head height at most, and the two-handed catch, can precede the practice.

2 Two hands to two hands has the cupped hands ready all the time. The cup closes round the bag and 'grabs it tight'. Demonstrate with someone who is really watching the bag carefully.

3 A teacher demonstration shows the long arm swinging 'forward, back, forward and throw' as the bean bag is aimed to land on one of the many lines or marks on the ground, at a distance of only 3 metres. The bag is picked up and another target is found.

Partner practices

1 After getting them into twos, ask one to put his or her bag down in the place where they were collected from. The one shared bag is handed into the hand of the partner, as they walk side by side, 'still keeping inside my playground classroom, please.'

2 Now they stand a very short distance (1 metre) apart, and aim to put the bean bag into their partner's outstretched hands.

3 The challenge 'Can you show me another way to send the bean bag to your partner?' is accompanied by much teacher commentary of the good things seen, and as a help to the less creative. This practice must be done gently, keeping very close together.

GROUP PRACTICES

1 Practice with the hoop includes using it on the ground for jumps and balances; holding it for spinning and bowling.

2 They 'take turns' at aiming to land the bean bag in the hoop, from about 2 metres.

3 In sending the big ball 'a little distance' we encourage much throwing up and catching, bouncing and catching, to keep ball near. Wild, long distance kicking, etc., must be discouraged.

Lesson Plan – 30 minutes

Emphasis on: (a) vigorous, whole body movements; (b) developing the habit of near continuous activity; (c) listening, while practising, and responding well to teaching.

WARM-UP AND FOOTWORK PRACTICES - 4 minutes

1 Can you run and jump over lines and show me your lively ways of landing, and then running on without stopping?

2 Can you try long jumps with a long, straight front leg?

3 Try a high jump now with the front knee bent and reaching high.

4 When I call 'Stop!' show me how quickly you can run into the box whose number I call out. (Teacher has numbered playground rectangles 1, 2, 3.)

SKILL PRACTICES: WITH HOOPS - 10 minutes

Individual practices

1 Put your hoop on the ground, nicely spaced away from others. Now run and jump in and out of all the hoops, without touching them (like stepping stones).

2 Can you run, jump up high, then do a nice, squashy landing into your own hoop?

3 Pick up your hoop and either try spinning it, or walk beside it, bowling it forward.

Partner practices

1 Show your partner something you like doing with your hoop, on the ground or in your hand. Your partner can either try to copy this or show you their favourite activity.

2 Can you and your partner hold your hoops and face each other, standing inside the hoop? Now try to roll the hoop sideways, still walking on the inside, very slowly and carefully. Can you keep going at the same speed, together?

GROUP PRACTICES - 16 minutes

1 Partners; bean bag each. Follow the leader who walks and shows you a simple activity with the bean bag. Following partner watches and tries to copy. (For example, throw and catch; balance on head or back of hand; kick up from top of shoe; bat up repeatedly.)

2 Hoop each. Can you do something lively with the hoop on the ground, and something where you hold it in one or both hands? ('Lively' - run and jump; hopscotch round; in hand, twist, throw and catch, bowl; skip with swing overhead.)

3 Small size ball each. Can you walk, throwing and catching, and try to do a quick hand clap between throw and catch? (Clap puts hands into good position for catches, near eyes, in front.) Can you try some one- and two-handed ways of throwing and catching, on the move?

Lesson Notes • 4 Lessons Development

WARM-UP AND FOOTWORK PRACTICES

1 Running and jumping, without stopping, is a great favourite with young children, and the lines give them a focus for their jumps.

2 The long, straight front leg in long jumping through the air can be demonstrated by the teacher or by one of the many children who will be doing this well. In a long jump you can see the foot of the front leg reaching out in front.

3 A high jump to lift you upwards has a bent front knee, reaching up as your arms are doing.

4 Class is shown the different, numbered rectangles and all call out the number of each one as they are introduced to it. They should then know where to race when a number is called.

SKILLS PRACTICES

Individual practices

1 After placing own hoop down in a space, they run and jump into and out of all the hoops, like playing 'stepping stones'.

2 Now they stop after each run and jump into a hoop to show a 'nice squashy landing' with a bending of the knees.

3 If bowling is too erratic, let them try to spin the hoop on the spot. With both, a teacher demonstration and explanation are essential. To start the bowling, hold the hoop upright at your right side if right-handed, with your left hand on top. The bowling hand is placed across the hoop away from you and pulls the hoop forward to make it roll.

Partner practices

1 The simplest partner work is always to 'Show your partner a favourite activity. Then your partner will demonstrate for you.' This allows the teacher to see the extent of the ability and the success of the teaching that has gone before.

2 The slow, sideways, balance walk inside the hoop is another activity that can be controlled and easily practised because both hands are helping. As a mirroring activity, it is good fun and gives pleasure when both manage to keep together.

GROUP PRACTICES

1 The friendly pleasure of partner work is experienced again, with a bean bag each, in 'Follow the leader'. 'Follow' infers going somewhere, so encourage them to keep moving - something that will be important, anyway, as the weather starts to become cooler. Balancing on hand or head; throwing up and catching; and throwing/aiming to land on a line, are all good activities.

2 Something 'lively' with the hoop means a big body action, either using the hoop on the ground for jumps or skips round; or bowling or skipping vigorously.

3 'Throw, clap, catch' using one hand for the throw, and two cupped hands for the catch, should be practised with eyes looking closely at the ball throughout, and with the ball being thrown no higher than head height, particularly when walking as well.

Lesson Plan – 30 minutes

Emphasis on: (a) enjoying the experience of vigorous physical activity; (b) practising wholeheartedly, almost without stopping, to become and stay warm, important as weather becomes colder in winter; (c) receiving and controlling, travelling with, and sending a ball.

WARM-UP AND FOOTWORK PRACTICES - 4 minutes

1 Show me your good, quiet running, as you visit all parts of our 'classroom'. Remember to lift heels and knees, and do not follow anyone.

2 When I call 'Stop!' show me your good running shape with your body leaning slightly forward, arms bent, and in a good space.

SKILL PRACTICES: WITH MEDIUM SIZE BALLS - 10 minutes

Individual practices

1 Can you walk, throwing and catching with both hands?

2 Can you throw the ball up in front, let it bounce, then catch it with two hands?

3 Now can you show me another way or ways to send the ball a little distance, collect it, then send it again (e.g. throw, roll, kick, head, bat, bounce)?

Partner practices

1 Walk side by side, handing the ball to each other, practising a good hand position for receiving (i.e. cupped, fingers forward).

2 Now can you walk, side by side, making a little throw to each other, with your hands ready, showing your partner where to aim?

3 Can you and your partner show me another way or ways that you can send the ball to each other (e.g. throw, bounce, roll, kick, head, bat, run and hand)?

GROUP PRACTICES - 16 minutes

1 Bean bag each. Walk round inside own space, throwing and catching. As you come to the line in front of the hoops, aim to throw bean bag into hoop (about 2 metres). Brisk walk around the rectangle circuit to keep warm. Walk, three or four catches, then aim.

2 Medium size ball between two. Send the ball a short distance to your partner. Can you keep on the move to keep warm as you kick, head, hand, bounce or throw your ball very carefully and gently. One could stand and other circle round for throw and catch with frequent changes. About 1 metre apart.

3 Ropes and hoops on the ground. Ropes lie straight, curved and in V shape. Hoops are scattered around among ropes. Group can run and jump in and out of hoops like stepping stones. You can jump from side to side over rope, across or along, or over Vs increasing width.

Lesson Notes • 4 Lessons Development

WARM-UP AND FOOTWORK PRACTICES

1 Good running is quiet and you don't run behind or follow anyone. Unless taught otherwise, young children all run in a big anti-clockwise circle, following everyone else. We ask them to 'visit every part of the playground classroom' to discourage the curving, anti-clockwise circle. By running on straight lines into corners, towards ends, sides and through the centre, the quality and variety of the running are greatly enhanced.

2 The slight lean of the whole body into the running with arms bent to allow a quick arm action to match the leg action, lets the class feel these positions.

SKILLS PRACTICES: WITH MEDIUM SIZE BALLS

Individual practices

1 From now on, right through the colder winter months, we ask for practising 'on the move' or 'walking', to try to maintain the body heat built up in the warm-up activities. Use both hands for throwing and catching at about head height where your eyes can see the ball well. Praise those who are 'throwing up carefully to head height only' and those who are 'really looking at the ball all the time.'

2 The throw up in front, usually with straight arms, is above head height, sufficient to allow the ball to bounce up to about waist height for the next catch.

3 Emphasise that the sending of the ball must be contained within our playground classroom, within the marked rectangle. Wild kicking or throwing must be stopped and replaced by careful, gentle throws, kicks, headers, bounces, rolls.

Partner practices

1 Side by side, walking and handing the ball to each other, lets them practise the correct receiving position of the hands with fingers spread on the sides, facing forward.

2 Still walking forward, the arms swing across you very slowly and gently and the ball is released just ahead of the partner who should be able to walk into the catch, grabbing the ball with both hands.

3 Other ways of partner sending and receiving, freely practised here, must be limited to 3 metres at most to ensure repetition and some chance of success.

GROUP PRACTICES

1 The brisk walking is done round the inside of the third of the whole area, approx. 20m x 10m, and each corner has a hoop as a target in which to aim to land the bean bag.

2 In sending the ball a short distance to a partner, on the move to keep warm, moving well to receive efficiently is as important as good sending.

3 Ask for interesting rope shapes on the ground to give ideas for lively running and jumping practices.

Lesson Plan – 30 minutes

Emphasis on: (a) warming up well with lots of vigorous leg activity; (b) chasing and dodging games; (c) almost uninterrupted practising of skills.

WARM-UP AND FOOTWORK PRACTICES - 5 minutes

1 Jog slowly through the ends of our playground 'classroom', and sprint quickly through the middle, watching carefully for others.

2 In jogging you are nearly upright with not too much lifting of heels and knees. In sprinting, you lean forward more and lift arms, heels and knees more.

3 All against all, 'tag' or 'he', trying not to be touched (caught) but also trying to touch as many others as possible. No hard pushing. Gentle touches only, for safety.

4 'Stop!' Who caught lots of others? Who wasn't caught at all?

SKILL PRACTICES: WITH BEAN BAGS OR QUOITS - 10 minutes

Individual practices

1 Jog round, making tiny throws and catches, watching bag or quoit carefully into your two hands, cupped ready.

2 Stand and make a little throw, up and a little way in front of you. Can you run and catch with hands nicely cupped again, and just in front of your eyes (about chest high)? Let your throw be like an aim with a long slow swing of your throwing arm, well up to give you time to get there. Catch with both hands.

Partner practices

1 Use one bean bag or quoit. Jog beside your partner and show me how you give quoit or bag to partner, trying not to drop it.

2 Can you stand, facing each other, about 1 metre apart? Use one hand to throw and two hands to catch, with your partner's hands showing you where to aim your careful throw (hands cupped).

3 With a bean bag or quoit each, standing about 3 metres apart (ideally on a line). One of you quietly say 'Ready ... aim!' and both will throw, aiming at partner's line, or next to where partner is standing. Then you run to change places, pick up your own bag or quoit, and the other partner calls 'Ready ... aim!'

GROUP PRACTICES - 15 minutes

1 Small ball each. Can you show me how you can play with ball freely, on the move? (Batting, heading, kicking, bouncing, rolling, throwing.) Keep moving, walking or jogging.

2 Bean bag or quoit with a partner. Standing about 2 metres apart, can you give each other a long arm swing aim and throw for a nice high catch? Do four, then sprint to change places.

3 Hoops 'tag'. Three chasers with coloured bands are allowed to catch you if you are not 'safe' in a hoop. If caught, take a band and start chasing.

Lesson Notes • 4 Lessons Development

WARM-UP AND FOOTWORK PRACTICES

1 In the end-to-end travelling, the class jog in the outside two thirds and sprint through the middle third, watching carefully for other sprinters coming towards them. A 'Keep to the left' might be a good idea if the area is narrow.

2 Jogging is an easy action with an upright body and little lift of heels or hands, and the steps are short. Sprinting at speed is done with a lean forward of the body weight, a strong lift of heels, knees and hands, and longer strides.

3 In dodging games like 'All against all tag', encourage good dodging actions such as direction changes rather than high speed racing away which leads to bumping and accidents.

SKILLS PRACTICES: WITH BEAN BAGS OR QUOITS

Individual practices

1 The jogging continues, to keep them warm, as they throw up with one and catch with two hands. Cupped hands which close round the bag or quoit, and eyes which watch the object closely at all times, are the main points to encourage, look for and praise.

2 From a standing start position, they throw the bean bag up and forward high enough to give them time to run to where the bag is coming down to catch it, standing still. The throw is with a long swing up of the throwing arm.

Partner practices

1 Still jogging, side by side, they are asked to give or send the bean bag or quoit to partner for an easy receipt, trying hard not to drop it.

2 Standing 2 to 3 metres apart only, a low one-hand swinging action is used to throw bean bag to partner's two cupped and outstretched hands. On receipt, close hands round the object and grab it in to yourself.

3 Partners stand apart on the side lines, or nearer if lines are too far apart. 'Ready ... aim!' is for both to respond to. Then they run to partner's side (keeping winter-warm) and repeat back to starting line with other partner giving the signal.

GROUP PRACTICES

1 Free practice with the small ball must be kept within the group's third of the area, and ideally will be practised 'on the move' to keep warm. Teacher commentary on and praise for the varied activities seen will extend the group's repertoire, as they use hands, feet, head in their varied ways.

2 At 2 metres apart, they should be able to succeed often with the long arm swing/aim as they send the bean bag or quoit to their partner who stands with cupped hands, forward and ready, as a target to aim for. 'Run to change places to keep warm.'

3 Last person caught starts the next game in which they all have a band on, except the chaser. When caught, take band off, put it down beside the other bands, and start chasing.

Lesson Plan – 30 minutes

Emphasis on: (a) wholehearted, safe and almost continuous action to keep warm; (b) developing simple, linked actions; (c) co-operating with a partner to improve and extend skills.

WARM-UP AND FOOTWORK PRACTICES - 5 minutes

1 Play follow the leader with your partner, and show me some lively running, jumping, hopping, skipping or bouncing actions.

2 Can you copy each other exactly, with your feet doing the same actions at the same time (i.e. mirroring, in unison)?

3 Now play tag or he with your partner. In this game you may only touch your partner when he or she is not on a line (i.e. on the line is safe, untouchable, but regular excursions from the lines are encouraged to keep them moving). Change duties often.

SKILL PRACTICES: WITH A SMALL BALL - 10 minutes

Individual practices

1 Jog round, holding your ball in cupped hands as if you had just caught it. Keep moving and looking for spaces to run into. When I call 'Change!' place your ball down, still, on the ground, leave it and find another ball to pick up and carry. I will be looking to see how quick you are. 'Change!' (Repeat several times.)

2 Change to walking, throwing and catching with two cupped hands, and fingers pointing forward. Can you keep a nice rhythm with your little throws, up and slightly in front of you? 'Throw, walk, catch; throw, walk, catch; throw, walk, catch.'

3 If your hands are cold; put them under your armpits and jog round, dribbling the ball like a footballer. Dribble a few times, then stop the ball by putting your foot on top of it.

Partner practices

1 Stand, facing your partner, two big steps apart. Throw with one hand and catch with two at three different heights: a low one, below the knees; a medium one to the waist; a higher one to chest.

2 Can you plan one or more ways to send the ball carefully to your partner, and keep moving to keep warm? (Side by side handing or throwing; football passing; one throwing, one heading; throwing up to let it bounce in front of the other, etc.)

GROUP PRACTICES - 15 minutes

1 Medium size ball with a partner. Send the ball to partner through the 2-metre space between bean bags (e.g. kicking, rolling, throwing, batting, heading).

2 Small ball each. Can you 'juggle' your ball, to keep it going up and bouncing? Strike with foot, head, thigh, front and back of hands.

3 Walking 'free and caught'. Three of group chase the seven others to catch them. When caught, stand still, hands on head, until 'set free' by someone touching elbows.

Lesson Notes • 4 Lessons Development

WARM-UP AND FOOTWORK PRACTICES

1 Partners could have been organised in the classroom to allow an instant start on arriving in the playground. Minimum waiting and maximum action are most important aims in mid-winter. They are told to follow the leader at a distance of about 2 metres so that the leader's actions and uses of feet can be seen easily.

2 If they can step, skip, run and jump, bounce, etc., at the same speed, copying step for step in unison, they deserve a special word of praise for effort and skilful observation.

3 Tag against a partner is made more interesting by the rule that you may only catch your partner when he or she is not on a line and 'safe'. When one is caught they change over duties.

SKILLS PRACTICES: WITH A SMALL BALL

Individual practices

1 Jogging and listening for 'Change!' is an example of an activity designed to develop attentive, quick responses. Ball is placed down gently on playground to prevent it rolling away. A different ball is found, picked up and the game continues.

2 Aim for a repeating rhythm and successful catching as they keep on the move, weaving in and out of one another. Ball is watched closely into hands which close round it to grab it in.

3 Football dribbling, with ball near enough to feet for instant stops, using inside, outside and laces parts of the shoe to stroke the ball forward or from side to side.

Partner practices

1 Couples stand 2 to 3 metres apart only, with one foot forward to help them to bend down for the low catches, below the knee. Throw is with a long, straight arm aiming at partner's outstretched and cupped hands.

2 Ball is sent only 2 to 3 metres from partner to partner to contain it in your third of the play area, to reduce time wasted chasing after wayward throws, and to provide the optimum practice time. Emphasise the importance of the receiving which is helped by moving early to be ready in place for the ball.

GROUP PRACTICES

1 Partners have to plan how to send the ball to pass through the small space between the two bean bags. The same or different methods may be used. One partner could bounce it through while the other partner could kick it through. If it is very cold, they can 'Do four, then run to change sides to start again.'

2 In juggling, the ball is struck upwards, then allowed to bounce once, then struck upwards, then allowed to bounce. This is a lively practice because players need to keep moving to get to the ball after each bounce to strike it up again.

3 Three chasers wear bands to identify them. They are told to touch gently without any dangerous pushing. Let game run for about 15 seconds, then change over the chasing trio.

Lesson Plan – 30 minutes

Emphasis on: (a) vigorous, immediate responses to become and stay winter-warm; (b) good footwork - dodging and chasing, and changing directions; (c) enjoying learning to control a big ball.

WARM-UP AND FOOTWORK PRACTICES - 5 minutes

1 Can you show me some lively ways you can travel to visit all parts of our playground 'classroom'? Are your actions so quiet that I would not hear you if I closed my eyes?

2 Mostly we go forwards but some movements can be done going sideways. Can you think of and show me any (e.g. slipping, skipping, bouncing)?

3 Free-and-caught with a quarter of the class wearing bands as chasers. If caught you stand still with hands on head. Those who are not caught can free you by touching you on the elbow. Changing direction suddenly is a good way to dodge. (Chasers are changed over often with comments on good performances.)

SKILL PRACTICES: WITH A LARGE BALL - 10 minutes

Individual practices

1 Walk or jog using two hands to throw the ball just above your head. Try to catch it with two hands just in front of your eyes (i.e. ball stays high). Thumbs behind and fingers well spread.

2 Keep walking and bounce the ball down just in front of you with both hands pushing. Catch the ball as it bounces back up.

3 Practise freely with your ball to show me how you can send it and then collect it. Remember to keep inside the lines of our 'classroom' (e.g. kick, throw, bounce, head, roll).

Partner practices

1 Stand facing your partner, about two big steps apart. Can one of you send the ball straight to your partner and the other one send it back with a little bounce between you (i.e. chest and bounce passes)? Use both hands each time, aiming carefully.

2 Like rugby players, can you jog side by side, and either throw a gentle, easy pass or hand it carefully to your partner?

3 Have some free practice, sending the ball to your partner in a favourite way that seems to work for the two of you.

GROUP PRACTICES - 15 minutes

1 Follow the leader with a choice of quoits, bean bags, hoops or balls. 'Follow' means going somewhere, moving to keep warm. Leader, do something simple.

2 Large ball with a partner. Can you invent a simple game? For example, throw for header; aim at line contest; kick to each other; chase to touch ball.

3 Free practice with a skipping rope, in one or both hands, or on the ground. Try skipping with a slow pull of rope along ground, or run and jump over rope.

Lesson Notes • 4 Lessons Development

WARM-UP AND FOOTWORK PRACTICES

1 The class repertoire of lively leg activities appropriate for warming up the body will include running; running and jumping; skipping; skipping with long, upward arm swings; bouncing with feet together; slipping steps sideways; and hopping.

2 Tell them that 'forward' means that the front of our body is going first. When we go 'sideways' one side of our body goes first.

'Backwards' should be done with great care and only for a few steps, while looking behind you over one shoulder.

3 Chasers are told to touch 'gently so that no-one is pushed over and hurt.' Dodgers are encouraged to dodge by using good footwork such as a change of direction, rather than high speed running away. Change the chasers every 15 seconds or so.

SKILLS PRACTICES: WITH A LARGE BALL

Individual practices

1 Ball is held in both hands, starting at head height and thrown to just above head height. They are asked to try to catch with both hands just in front of the eyes where ball can be seen right into the hands.

2 Two-handed bouncing to bring ball up to waist height for an easy, two-handed catch, should be tried 'on the move' by reaching forward to bounce it down to come up for you to walk on to.

3 Ask for 'little' throws, kicks, headers, bounces, rolls, batting to lessen the number of runaway balls.

Partner practices

1 The straight chest pass is aimed at your partner's chest. The bounce pass is aimed just in front of partner's feet.

2 Whether throwing or handing the ball, they run almost shoulder to shoulder to make the pass as easy as possible.

3 Free practice at 2 to 3 metres apart is ideally done on the move, so should be something they find quite easy.

GROUP PRACTICES

1 On alternate weeks, they can be the leader and decide the equipment to be used. 'Following' means going somewhere which we hope means keeping warm, particularly if the activity is simple for the sake of successful repetition. 2 metres apart lets the follower have a good look at the leader's action or actions.

2 The 'simple game' which they are challenged to invent for two players with one ball, can be a simple practice of a skill or a little 1 v 1 competition, e.g. throw up to self to head it past partner on a line; aim to throw it past partner, guarding a line; run after partner to touch ball held by him or her.

3 Skipping rope on ground can be jumped over or bounced along, from side to side or above. A held rope can be used to learn to skip by turning rope overhead to hit ground and slide towards you, for a step over. Skippers are asked to show their best skipping, sometimes on the spot, sometimes on the move.

Lesson Plan – 30 minutes

Emphasis on: (a) an enthusiastic response to the challenge to try out new activities; (b) varied ways to use a skipping rope; (c) co-operation with a partner.

WARM-UP AND FOOTWORK PRACTICES - 5 minutes

1 In your running, can you show me a good lifting of knees, heels to make it quiet? Remember to run along straight lines, never following anyone. (Primary school children run in an anti-clockwise circle, following each other, if not taught otherwise.)

2 Five points tag. All have five points to start with. All chase and dodge away from all. If 'tagged' by someone, you lose one of your starting five points.

3 'Stop!' Who was a good dodger and kept four or five points? Who was a good chaser and caught more than three others? (Repeat.)

SKILL PRACTICES: WITH SKIPPING ROPES - 10 minutes

Individual practices

1 Place rope flat and straight on ground. Jump, skip or hop from side to side along and back. Can you make up a little rhythm as you go? 'Jump over, then bounce; jump over, then bounce; hop, 2, 3 and turn.'

2 Make a circle shape on the ground. Can you jump right across, or into and out of, or do a big high jump into it?

3 Pick up your rope and try skipping freely. (Those who can not skip yet can skip along, rope in one hand at side, turning the rope to hit the ground.)

Partner practices

Jump the wriggling snake. One partner, with rope, crouches down and makes the long rope wriggle up and down in waves on the ground with a strong wrist action. Running and jumping partner crosses rope from both sides. Change over often.

GROUP PRACTICES - 15 minutes

1 Small ball with a partner. Can you and your partner invent a simple little game to practise throwing and catching?

2 Skipping rope each. Practise freely, trying to skip on the move, pulling the rope slowly over to slide towards you to step over, if just learning. (Better ones, on the spot and moving.)

3 Partners. One hoop and five bean bags. Each has five aims to land the bean bags in the hoop, from a line about 3 metres away. What is your best team score out of ten?

Lesson Notes • 4 Lessons Development

WARM-UP AND FOOTWORK PRACTICES

1 Short bursts of flat-footed, noisy running followed by running on tiptoes with a good feeling of lifting heels and knees, will let the class hear what is and what is not wanted. By now their running should be well established as straight line running, never circling or following others, with visits to all parts of the teaching space.

2 Depending on the class subtraction ability level, the five points from which they subtract one each time they are caught (i.e. touched gently by another) may need to be changed to four or three.

3 Stop the game after 15 seconds to calm them down, check on 'Who is a good dodger and still has five points? Who is a good chaser and caught three or more?'

SKILLS PRACTICES: WITH SKIPPING ROPES

Individual practices

1 Ropes are well spaced out, lying straight on the ground. Lively end-to-end skipping, jumping, hopping or bouncing is helped by a feeling of rhythm within the short sequence.

2 A circle shape challenges them to leap across or to run, jump and land inside. Which is your jumping-off foot? Can you jump up from two feet sometimes? Can you do a nice, squashy landing?

3 Trying to skip can be the real thing with overhead pulls of the rope, or simply running with the rope at one side in one hand which turns the rope in a circle as you run along.

Partner practices

The wriggling snake, waving up and down in ripples just above ground level, is unpredictable with interesting highs and lows to leap over.

GROUP PRACTICES

1 They can simply create a co-operative practice, throwing and catching in some way, or they can make a little competitive, 1 v 1 game which involves them in deciding how to score and how to re-start after a score, e.g. one counts his or her throws and catches on the spot while partner races to touch a mark on the playground, ideally about a 15-metre run. When runner comes back the counting partner stops counting and tells partner how many catches were made. Change duties and the new thrower and catcher tries for a better score.

2 Free practice with a skipping rope lets them continue with the earlier practising, including trying skipping with the overhead pull, or activities with the rope on the ground.

3 They 'take turns' at throwing five bean bags to try to land them in the hoop which is 2 or 3 metres away. The secret of good aiming is to use a long, straight arm action to throw high enough to let the bean bag see the hoop.

Lesson Plan – 30 minutes

Emphasis on: (a) the athletic activities of running, jumping and throwing; (c) increasing body control and self-confidence; (c) enjoying experimenting with a variety of implements.

WARM-UP AND FOOTWORK PRACTICES - 5 minutes

1 Can you do a big high jump over a line and show me which is your jumping-off foot?

2 You don't need to run fast to jump high. Show me a nice, springy push and let your front knee reach up high.

3 Four lines relay. Partners stand side by side anywhere inside the lines of the teaching area. On signal, 'A' races to touch the outside four lines (two ends, two sides) of the teaching space, and back to touch partner 'B' who repeats the run.

SKILL PRACTICES: WITH BEAN BAGS - 10 minutes

Individual practices

1 Walk, finding good spaces, throwing up low to about chest height; medium to about head height; and higher to just above head.

2 Walk, balancing the bean bag on the back of your outstretched hand. Throw it up gently to catch it with the front of your hand. Can you do this balance-throw-catch using both left and right hands?

3 All on one side line. Throw underarm to make your bean bag go as near to the opposite side line as possible. Run after it. Take it on to the opposite line and repeat back to starting line. Use a long swing forward, back, forward and throw each time.

Partner practices

1 Stand very close to your partner, about a metre apart. Throw the bean bag to each other a few times. Now move back one step and throw again, about 2 metres apart, a few times. Have one more move back to about 3 metres and throw and catch carefully again.

2 Partners stand on opposite side lines. Using an underarm action, can you throw the bean bag to land in front of your partner on his or her side line? This long aim and throw is helped by a long swing forward, back and forward with a straight arm.

GROUP PRACTICES - 15 minutes

1 Free practice with a choice of ropes, hoops, balls or quoits. Can you show me your favourite activities with one piece of equipment? Practise continuously by yourself to improve.

2 Partners with one bean bag at a line or rope 'net'. How long a rally can you and your partner make before dropping it? Throw with one hand to partner's two outstretched hands.

3 Partners with one medium or large ball. Try to keep moving as you show me ways to travel with, send and receive your ball. Hands and feet both important.

Lesson Notes • 4 Lessons Development

WARM-UP AND FOOTWORK PRACTICES

1 Encourage a springy upward movement in high jumping with the feeling of lifting arms, head and leading knee straight up.

2 The feeling is of rocking up into the jump from a heel, ball, toes action in the take-off foot.

3 In four lines sprint relay race, partners both start and finish at the same place. Each of four surrounding lines of the playground 'classroom' must be touched with a shoe, before racing back to touch partner. To help teacher identify winning couples, children are asked to finish 'Standing side by side, still.'

SKILLS PRACTICES: WITH BEAN BAGS

Individual practices

1 Throw up with one hand and catch with two, ideally at about mid-chest height where bean bag can be well watched. The three different heights give practice in judging the effort needed to achieve these different heights.

2 Walking, balancing, throwing and catching is an enjoyable example of 'joining skills together with increasing control.'

3 The swing 'forward, back and forward' of the throwing arm is important to achieve a controlled and repeating throw and aim at a target line. Sufficient height is needed to 'let the bean bag see the line' and carry it to the target.

Partner practices

1 Repeat the practising at one width several times so that your body can 'remember' how to do it at that distance. Move a little further apart, and repeat, discovering how much more effort and height are needed this time. One more move back and a final practice, aiming, catching and looking very carefully.

2 The cross court aiming at your partner's line develops accuracy through straighter throwing, and judgements of force and height needed to cover a set distance. Repeated practice aims to develop skill and 'muscle memory.'

GROUP PRACTICES

1 Free practice with a choice of implements is provided to enable more practice of skills that are enjoyed and can be practised almost non-stop to become even more skilful and satisfying. Teacher challenges can lead to greater quality and variety. 'Can you spin the hoop on parts of your body or on the ground?'

2 Co-operative throwing and catching of a bean bag over a 'net' is practised at about 2 metres apart only. Quoit is carefully swung forward, back and forward each time, aiming at partner's hands, outstretched as a target.

3 In sending a big ball to a partner, emphasise sending it a short distance, keeping in the allocated area always, not disturbing other groups. Neat, well controlled, repeatable practising is looked for, with the ball seldom wandering out of control.

Lesson Plan – 30 minutes

Emphasis on: (a) working carefully and thoughtfully, almost without stopping, to practise to improve; (b) learning to judge force and height when batting a small ball by oneself and with a partner; (c) planning to link simple actions together.

WARM-UP AND FOOTWORK PRACTICES - 5 minutes

1 Run and jump over the lines without touching them. I would like to see long and high jumps, pretending each line is a low wall which you have to clear.

2 When I call 'Stop!' show me how quickly you can stand, balanced up on tiptoes, on the nearest line. Stop! (Repeat.)

SKILL PRACTICES: WITH SMALL BATS AND BALLS - 10 minutes

Individual practices

1 Can you walk, balancing the ball on the flat bat?

2 Stand, hit the ball straight up a little way, let it bounce, then hit it up again.

3 Try to walk, using the bat like a big hand, striking the ball down just in front of you. Use your wrist only.

Partner practices

1 Can you try, both with a bat, or one with a bat and one using a hand, to strike the ball straight up between you, then let it bounce, then hit it up. Keep your best score of 'Strike it up, let it bounce.'

2 One with bat and ball drops ball to let it bounce up and very gently bats it for partner to receive and hand back to batter. Have four or five hits each, very gently and slowly, 'feeling' how much power to give it.

GROUP PRACTICES - 15 minutes

1 Skipping rope each. Practise skipping, on the spot or on the move. If you are just learning, use a long, slow overhead pull to make it slide along the ground for you to step over. Use a very small turn of your wrists.

2 Bat and ball each. Can you plan to do something on the spot and something where you are moving? Be gentle with your hitting and use your wrists, not your elbows or shoulders. Watch the ball well, hitting it just in front of your eyes.

3 Partners; hoop each. Can you show your partner either some balancing, walking on the hoop on the ground, or in hands? Can you skip; with the hoop in one or both hands? You can swing the hoop forwards and back, and from side to side.

Lesson Notes • 4 Lessons Development

WARM-UP AND FOOTWORK PRACTICES

1 To encourage flight, elevation, height, ask them to pretend that each line is a low wall to be cleared. This should encourage a good sprint into a long jump and a springy action into a high jump. Children can be asked to think about 'Which foot do you push off with in your high jumps and your long jumps?'

2 A quick response to 'Stop!' is always a good exercise because it trains a quick response to a signal or instruction. With a good class there should be no more than a 2 second gap between 'Stop!' and all being stationary, balanced on tiptoes.

SKILLS PRACTICES; WITH SMALL BATS AND BALLS

Individual practices

1 Bat is held at mid-chest height, with a well bent arm for good vision and control.

2 Bouncing upwards to about head height is produced by a gentle wrist action. The elbow and the shoulder do not join in.

3 Little hands should hold the bat near to its face and the fingers can even spread over part of the back of the face to help the feeling that the bat is an extension of the hand. Ball is struck firmly enough to bounce it up to about waist level.

Partner practices

1 Partners stand within touching distance of each other, trying to make the ball bounce vertically between them up to about waist height. Bat, or hand if preferred, strikes gently under the ball, 'feeling' how much force is necessary. One bounce between hits is the aim, but more than one bounce between is helpful.

2 This challenging practice for a Reception class needs to be at no more than 3 metres apart. Receiving partner needs to have both cupped hands reaching forward, ready to catch, and to show partner where to aim.

GROUP PRACTICES

1 Learner skippers can run round with rope in one hand and practise the turning action at one side, then move on to the long, slow, overhead pull, with both hands, to make the longish rope land well ahead before sliding along the ground towards you, to step over.

2 Bat and ball practice gives another opportunity to practise the skills which very young children find difficult. 'Feel' and hand and eye co-ordination are being developed. Success in making short rallies is a source of great satisfaction. 'I can do three! Come and see me!'

3 As a balance to the individual and difficult rope and bat and ball, group practices, partner activities with a hoop allow them to co-operate, demonstrate and learn from each other. Balancing, bowling or skipping are big favourites.

Equipment: 30 small bats and balls; ten skipping ropes, ten hoops.

Lesson Plan – 30 minutes

The emphasis is on: (a) neat, controlled actions developed by listening well to class teaching; (b) practising in a well planned way; (c) co-operating with a partner to develop good footwork and ball control skills.

WARM-UP AND FOOTWORK PRACTICES - 5 minutes

1 Follow your leader who will show you walking, running, jumping or other ways to travel. Watch the actions carefully and try to show me a little sequence of two or three joined together which you can repeat.

2 Now the other partner will lead. Keep together and listen for the number I call out (corresponding to one of the numbered areas of the playground). Let's see which couple is first, and last, to arrive in that numbered area. Number . . . two!

SKILL PRACTICES: WITH SMALL BALLS - 10 minutes

Individual practices

1 Throw up and catch with both hands well cupped, fingers pointing away from you. Can you catch the ball just in front of your eyes and let your hands 'give' to stop the ball bouncing out?

2 Walk, batting the ball up a little way in front of you with one hand. Let it bounce up, then bat it again. Bat; let bounce; bat up.

3 Roll the ball forward, run after it, crouch to pick up with one hand. Turn and repeat back to starting place. This is called 'fielding' the ball.

Partner practices

1 Stand, facing your partner, about two big steps apart. Throw to your partner's cupped hands reaching forward as a target. Let your catching hands 'give' to stop the ball bouncing out again.

2 Can you and your partner stand close together and bat the ball straight up between you with gentle, careful strikes? What is your best score?

3 Now roll the ball to your partner (4 metres apart) for him or her to bend down to field, pick up and then roll to you.

GROUP PRACTICES - 15 minutes

1 Partners; quoits. Play one with one, throwing over a low rope 'net', or one against one, to try to make it land on partner's side for a point. Throw with one, catch with two hands.

2 Partners; small ball. Aim your ball to land between two marks, cones or bean bags, then bounce up for your partner to catch. Now try to roll it between the markers, for partner to field.

3 Bat and ball each. Can you balance your ball on your bat? Now hit it up two or three times, then catch it, still, on bat. Walk, batting ball down and just in front of you.

Lesson Notes • 4 Lessons Development

WARM-UP AND FOOTWORK PRACTICES

Emphasise that the leader must give the couple good space to travel through, and to try to visit all parts of the playground 'classroom'. Leader thinks actions and should be able to say what two or three actions he or she plans to include.

A smooth linking of the actions is to be encouraged, particularly if there is an attractive variety, e.g. slow, straight leg running; lively, well bent knees, galloping; and tiptoe walking.

SKILLS PRACTICES: WITH SMALL BALLS

Individual practices

1 Encourage class to look closely at the ball and be able to say something about it - its colour; texture; any markings, etc. - so that they are concentrating on it right into their hands.

2 Bat up, let bounce, bat up, is done with a soft, gentle action in the wrist, 'feeling' how little force is needed to send it to the right height and distance ahead.

3 In fielding a rolling ball, we run to a position beside the ball, facing the direction the ball is travelling with ball on good hand side. Crouch to pick it up. A common fault is to run sideways beside the ball to try to go past it.

Partner practices

1 Make sure they stand very close together, almost close enough to touch outstretched, cupped hands. The 'giving' in the hands is easily practised at this close range, and can be the emphasis.

2 Standing even closer, bat the ball vertically up between you with a soft, gentle wrist action. Aim to make the ball bounce up to about waist height of your partner for the next hit.

3 In fielding a ball rolling towards you, turn half to one side with one foot forward, one back on throwing hand side, and crouch down to pick it up.

GROUP PRACTICES

1 Partner quoits. Gently aim and throw over the low rope 'net', or paint line. Partner is only about 2 metres away with both hands reaching forward to show thrower where to aim with one hand. The preparatory arm swing forward, back, then forward and throw, is important.

2 Small ball partners practice is done at about 2 metres apart, to make the aiming and the catching more successful, more often. At this close distance the aiming will be an underarm action.

3 Three different bat and ball practices for variety. Balance it on bat at chest height. Try gentle hits up a short distance and then try to catch it, balanced again. Walk, using bat like a big hand to hit ball down on to ground. In all striking, emphasise that the wrist is used to move the bat, not the elbow or shoulders which produce excessively strong movements.

Equipment: 30 small balls; five quoits; ten small balls; long rope 'net'.

Lesson Plan – 30 minutes

Emphasis on: (a) demonstrating, as always, enthusiastic and vigorous participation; (b) demonstrating a positive attitude which implies 'These lessons are fun, interesting, exciting and good for us'; (c) displaying a pleasing end of year level of variety and quality.

WARM-UP AND FOOTWORK PRACTICES - 5 minutes

1 Show me good, quiet, straight ahead running with body, legs, arms and shoulders all pointing straight ahead. (No side to side twisting action.)

2 Remember that good running is also quiet and you don't follow anyone. Run on straight lines, not curves.

3 Partners stand side by side down middle of court. On signal, one races to touch a side line, then races back to touch partner's hand as signal to race to touch other line. Repeat.

SKILL PRACTICES: WITH SKIPPING ROPES - 10 minutes

Individual practices

1 On the spot, all turn the rope over your head with a long, slow arm action. The rope hits the ground well in front of you, slides towards you and you can step over it. All practise this way to learn skipping, and use only a small wrist action.

2 Those who are able to skip well can try travelling forward with a running action to take you over your rope. Still make it land in front of you, to slide towards you, slowly.

Partner practices

1 If you are both learning, try to stand, side by side, and do the slow, overhead pull together, at the same speed.

2 If you are both good skippers, play follow the leader, keeping well apart, and well away from all other skippers.

GROUP PRACTICES - 15 minutes

1 Free practice with a partner with choice of balls, hoops, quoits, ropes, bat and ball. Can you and your partner show me some neat, quiet actions with your choice of equipment? Do something simple that you can keep repeating.

2 Skipping rope each. Practise freely, on the spot or moving. Can you skip with a bounce, feet together, and sometimes with a running action, one foot after the other?

3 One bean bag among three; 'piggy in the middle'. Pairs throw the bean bag to each other, trying to keep it away from the opponent in the middle. Pairs must be no more than 2-3 metres apart to make good throws and easy catches.

Lesson Notes • 4 Lessons Development

WARM-UP AND FOOTWORK PRACTICES

1 The 'straight ahead' style refers both to the look of the body and the pathways being followed, in good running. Emphasise here how the hands (and, therefore, the shoulders) reach forward and back, straight. The class can practise running along some of the lines, with feet pointing along the line, and arms keeping parallel to the line.

2 The emphasis here is on the route being followed. Always run in a straight ahead fashion, with a direction change to a new straight line when you find yourself following another, or are at a side line.

3 In side line sprint relay, emphasise that they touch on or over the line with a foot. Race can last for 'Four!' or 'Five!' or more side line touches. At the end the teacher calls out the names of the winning couples.

SKILLS PRACTICES: WITH SKIPPING ROPES

Individual practices

1 This slow motion practice is with a rope that is quite long, coming up to chest height when you stand on it. Learn to do it on the spot, stepping over the rope slowly sliding along the ground towards you. Turning hands are at about shoulder height.

2 Progress to the same action 'on the move', still stepping over the longish rope sliding towards you along the ground.

Partner practices

1 Standing side by side, facing opposite directions, about 1 metre apart and keeping together in their 'Step over; step over; step over', is an enjoyable, co-operative, partner activity.

2 In follow the leader, skipping, you must stay far enough behind the leader to avoid entangling him or her with your rope. Space between the pair and space for the pair are important.

GROUP PRACTICES

1 In free practice with a partner, the aim is for near continuous practice at something that needs two for its performance, co-operating or competing.

2 While it is free practice with a skipping rope each, the teacher will continually be praising good work, commenting on examples of variety, and challenging them to try something more adventurous, always in pursuit of a greater class repertoire.

3 The typical method of playing is to stand, far apart, and throw the bean bag over the head of the one in the middle. Try to keep the throwing pair only 2-3 metres apart, so that a good throw and catch are possible. The difficulty lies in encouraging the receiver to 'move sideways and forward into a space' to receive the bean bag, unimpeded by the one in the middle. If necessary, ask the 'piggy' to be passive to help the throwers succeed.

Equipment: 30 skipping ropes; five bean bags; 'free choice' selection.

Lesson Plan – 30 minutes

Emphasis at start of new school year on: (a) establishing a tradition of almost non-stop, wholehearted and enthusiastic participation, supported by (b) instant responses to instructions and signals, and (c) experiencing pleasure through participation in activity.

WARM-UP AND FOOTWORK PRACTICES - 4 minutes

1 Good running is quiet and you don't follow anyone. Show me your best running with a good lifting of heels, knees, arms and chest.

2 Run straight, not curving, and try to visit every part of our playgound 'classroom'. (Primary school children will all run in an anticlockwise circle, unless taught not to do so.)

3 When I call 'Stop!', be in a space all by yourself, standing perfectly still. Stop! (Demand the immediate response that this activity is designed for.)

SKILL PRACTICES: WITH SMALL BATS AND BALLS - 10 minutes

Individual practices

1 Can you balance your ball on the bat? Now can you bat the ball upwards very gently?

2 Try walking slowly forward, alternately balancing and hitting the ball a little way upwards.

3 Bat the ball up and in front of you, let it bounce up, then bat it up again. Be very gentle, using your wrist to move the bat, not elbow or shoulder. What is your best score?

Partner practices

1 One using the bat, one using a hand, can you keep the ball going up and down with one bounce on the ground in between? What is your best score, non-stop? Let other partner try with the bat.

2 One with bat strikes ball carefully for partner to catch. Ball can be dropped, then hit, or hit from hand. Stand only 3 metres apart with catcher's hands reaching well forward as a target.

GROUP PRACTICES - 16 minutes

1 Small bat and ball each. Practise freely on the spot and moving. A little sequence, standing then moving, would be interesting (e.g. bat up, standing, bat down, walking).

2 Partners with a bean bag. 2-3 metres apart, throw and catch, low (below knees), medium (to chest), higher (just above head). Throw with one hand, catch with two.

3 Hoop each. Show me ways to use the hoop, sometimes on the ground, sometimes in one or both hands (e.g. balancing round, on ground, and bowl or skip in hand or hands).

Lesson Notes • 4 Lessons Development

WARM-UP AND FOOTWORK PRACTICES

1 Running may be a completely natural activity but it will be done very badly unless good practice is explained and insisted upon. Noisy, flat-footed clumping round is often seen and a silent demonstration by the teacher or a small group of pupils will have an immediate effect, particularly if the teacher says 'I am going to close my eyes while you are practising. I do not want to hear a sound.'

2 All primary school children run in an anti-clockwise circle, all following one another, unless taught to 'Run on straight lines, never following anyone. Visit all parts of the space, the ends, the sides, the middle, the corners, never curving.'

3 The command to be standing, still, in a space, well away from all others, is an exercise in responding to a signal (immediately!) and in thinking about own and others' space.

SKILLS PRACTICES; WITH SMALL BATS AND BALLS

Individual practices

1 Because of traditional good weather in September, we can have a bat and ball lesson. Batting skills are difficult and tend to be rather static, so they are done in warmer weather. To help with the balancing and hitting the children are asked to hold their bat or racket near the head, not at the end of the handle.

2 With a bent arm they will have greater control and can hold the bat near, where their eyes can see the ball well, just in front of their faces.

3 The hit up is high enough to let the ball bounce on the ground and come up to waist height for the next strike. The movement takes place in the wrist, not the elbow or shoulder.

Partner practices

1 Partners stand close enough to touch each other. The practice starts with the ball being dropped between them on to the ground by one partner. The other partner hits under the ball to strike it vertically upwards to bounce for the next hit by the other partner. Good footwork takes the player to the correct spot each time.

2 Batter chooses to hit from the hand as in table tennis or to drop for a bounce up for the hit. Catcher's outstretched hands show the batter where to aim.

GROUP PRACTICES

1 Free practice allows a reinforcement of some of the difficult skills of balancing, striking and judging force. Alternating on the spot with on the move leads to interesting and challenging sequences and linking skills together.

2 Sending and receiving are easily and pleasantly practised with a bean bag which is easy to grab and does not bounce away.

3 The hoop can be on the ground for jumps and balances, and in the hands for skipping, spinning and bowling.

Lesson Plan – 30 minutes

Emphasis on: (a) continuing to establish the habit of practising quietly and listening to the teaching while practising; (b) good sharing of space and awareness of others for safe, satisfactory and enjoyable practice.

WARM-UP AND FOOTWORK PRACTICES - 4 minutes

1 Can you run, looking for spaces to run through?

2 Run very slowly, or even on the spot, if you are near others. Go faster when you see a big space.

3 When I call 'Stop!' show me how quickly you can run and jump to land and stand, perfectly still on tiptoes, on one of the lines.

SKILL PRACTICES: WITH HOOPS - 10 minutes

Individual practices

1 Put your hoop on the ground, nicely spaced away from others. Now run and jump in and out of all hoops, without touching them, like stepping stones.

2 Can you run and jump high and do a nice, squashy landing into any empty hoop. Are you jumping up with one or both feet?

3 Now lift up a hoop and practise freely using one or both hands (e.g. bowling, spinning, skipping, throwing and catching).

Partner practices

1 Partner tag, where the chaser may only touch their partner when the partner is not 'safe' in a hoop.

2 Now show your partner something you enjoy doing with your hoop. Then your partner will show you and you might learn a new skill. You might even be able to perform it at the same time.

GROUP PRACTICES - 16 minutes

1 Large ball each. Practise throwing and catching on the move. Can you throw low (waist), medium (chest) and high (above head)? Use two hands for throw and catch. Watch ball all the way into your reaching, cupped hands.

2 Partners; with a hoop. Can you and your partner invent an activity where you can mirror each other in some way? For example, one each side, bowling one hoop; walking sideways inside own hoop, holding it in two hands; both bowl to each other at same time from 2 metres.

3 Skipping rope each. Practise freely, but try some on the spot and some on the move. Can you do a double beat of your feet for each turn of the rope? Can you go forward, running one foot after the other?

WARM-UP AND FOOTWORK PRACTICES

1 Good sharing of space reduces accidents and frustration and lets you practise in a satisfactory way. Such sharing is safe and sociable.

2 We have to learn to adjust to the space available, slowing down when near others and speeding up when there is lots of room.

3 The signal to 'Stop!' and then run and jump to land on the nearest line, perfectly still on tiptoes, is an exercise in being attentive and responding immediately to instructions.

SKILLS PRACTICES: WITH HOOPS

Individual practices

1 The 25–30 hoops of a typical class are spaced out to create sets of 'stepping stones' near enough for a series of steps and spread wide for running and jumping.

2 Try one- and two-footed take-offs as you jump up high to land with a 'squashy' action and a 'give' in the knees. The landing can be with both feet or with one foot, then the other.

3 Free, but guided practice, with hoop in hand or hands encourages a variety of class responses including the quite easy spinning on the ground, wrist, ankle or waist; the quite difficult bowling and walking beside the hoop; and the very difficult skipping, either low from side to side, or overhead.

Partner practices

1 With lots of hoops to 'hide' in as safe havens, dodging partners have to be encouraged to be 'good sports' and not linger too long in the hoop. When caught the dodger becomes the chaser.

2 It is hoped that the watching partner will say something complimentary to the partner who has just demonstrated a favourite activity. It is also hoped that many of the watchers will learn something new to try.

GROUP PRACTICES

1 Habitual practising 'on the move' becomes important from now on as the weather starts to become colder. Throwing to oneself on the move, using both hands, is best done throwing straight upwards. The challenge to throw to different heights gives practice in 'feeling' how much effort to put into a variety of throws. Receiving is as important as the sending and a good hand position, cupped with fingers spread forward, is needed.

2 To plan or 'invent' a game or a practice is an important element with NC as are the performing and the reflecting/evaluating. This sociable and creative activity brings great pleasure to the participants, and can add something new to the class repertoire.

3 Most Year 1 children are able to learn how to skip if given enough opportunities. A long, slow overhead pull to make the rope slide towards you for a step over, is stage one. Hands are wide and the turn of the rope is made with a small wrist action.

Lesson Plan – 30 minutes

Emphasis on: (a) the pleasure of working with a partner; (b) the good feeling when your improvement and achievement are recognised, praised and often used to help others to improve.

WARM-UP AND FOOTWORK PRACTICES - 5 minutes

1 Play follow the leader with a partner where the leader does a short, easy-to-copy walk, then run, then jump. Is there something special about the walk (e.g. straight legs), the run (e.g. with high knee raising), the jump (e.g. with a half turn to finish)?

2 Five points tag. All have five points to start with. Each time you are caught by someone touching you, you lose a point. (No dangerous pushing - touch gently.)

SKILL PRACTICES: WITH BEAN BAGS - 10 minutes

Individual practices

1 Walk forward, throwing up, clapping hands, then catching. The hand clap puts your hands in a good position for a catch, cupped and high in front of your eyes.

2 Throw up, not very high, and catch (about head height). Throw up higher and catch (just above head height). Now throw up as high as you think you can catch. If you can do all that on the move, that will be excellent.

Partner practices

1 Stand close and try underhand throwing with one hand, catching with two hands. Catcher, hold your hands, forward and cupped, where you want your partner to aim. Thrower, swing forward, back and then throw with a long arm swing.

2 Can you walk or jog, side by side, and gently throw the bean bag to your partner, just in front of him or her, and high enough for an easy catch?

3 Stand about 3 metres apart with one foot forward towards your partner. Try to aim the bean bag to land on your partner's front foot. Keep your own score of good hits.

GROUP PRACTICES - 15 minutes

1 Partners; with a medium or large ball. One partner will decide on simple ways to travel as a pair with the ball. The other partner will then decide ways to send and receive the ball.

2 Bean bag among three; piggy in the middle. Two against one with the two throwing the bean bag to each other to keep it away from the

one. Throwers keep moving about 3 metres apart, to give one a chance.

3 Small ball each. Practise 'juggling' to keep the ball up, bouncing once in between strikes with different body parts. Move quickly to be ready for the next strike upwards. What is your best score?

Lesson Notes • 4 Lessons Development

WARM-UP AND FOOTWORK PRACTICES

1 The teacher can introduce this activity by having everyone working to his or her rhythm to show that each part is short. 'Ready? All walking . . . all running . . . now jump. 'This stops individuals walking or running long distances, instead of getting on with creating a short sequence.

2 Subtraction ability levels in Year 1 should enable them to play this game and keep their own score during the 15-20 seconds of each game before the teacher calls 'Stop!' Who dodged well and still has five points? Who chased well and caught three or more others?'

SKILLS PRACTICES: WITH BEAN BAGS

Individual practices

1 From now until the end of the spring term we aim to keep the children moving to keep warm. The throwing and catching of the bean bag, therefore, is done on the move. Most of the teaching is also done while the class is practising. A good demonstration will be very short. 'Watch how Jane looks at the bean bag very closely right into her cupped hands which are just in front of her eyes.' (10–15 seconds and all start working again.)

2 Throws to low, to medium, and to high give experience in 'feeling' how little or how much effort is needed to produce the varied results. Too much effort is the usual fault.

Partner practices

1 The swing forward, back, then forward swing/aim/throw is done with along, straight arm. Catcher's outstretched and cupped hands give thrower a target to aim at and focus on.

2 Rugby style carrying and throwing with both hands swinging across the body is done almost side by side to ensure easy, successful practice. Bean bag is aimed just ahead of the partner for him or her to run on to.

3 In aiming the bag to land on your partner's foot, throw it high enough to cover the distance and try to remember how much force and speed your good ones needed.

GROUP PRACTICES

1 Thinking and *planning* is needed to invent ways to *travel* with the ball, as a pair, and to *send and receive* as a pair. A brief demonstration by the groups after their turn at this activity is recommended because of the important NC requirements being pursued.

2 When the 'piggy' who was in the middle intercepts the bean bag someone else takes a turn in the middle. The two doing the throwing and catching need to be encouraged to move to the side into a space to be able more easily to receive the next throw.

3 Start by dropping the ball on to the ground to make it bounce straight upwards. Then hit the ball up with a body part; let it bounce; hit it up; and keep your best score. Five is excellent.

Lesson Plan – 30 minutes

Emphasis on: (a) travelling with, sending, and receiving a large ball; (b) responding enthusiastically to challenges.

WARM-UP AND FOOTWORK PRACTICES - 5 minutes

1 Run freely and change direction when I call 'Change!' Push hard with one foot to make yourself go the other way.

2 Play tag or he with your partner. You may only catch your partner when he or she is not 'safe' on a line (i.e. on a line is untouchable, but encourage regular excursions; change duties often).

SKILL PRACTICES: WITH A LARGE BALL - 10 minutes

Individual Practices

1 Throw up with both hands, then catch, walking. Aim to throw ball up to about head height and just in front of you for an easy catch just in front of eyes. Hands are cupped ready.

2 Throw ball up and a little bit in front of you to bounce on ground. Run after it and catch with both hands after the bounce.

3 Now show me another way to send the ball a little distance, then collect it and send it again (e.g. kick, head, roll, bounce).

Partner practices

1 Stand about 2 metres apart. Thrower, throw ball slightly to one side of your partner who has to move quickly to collect it.

2 Now use both hands to bounce the ball just in front of your partner for a catch. Make it bounce about 1 metre in front of him or her.

3 Can you invent a standing practice for sending the ball to a partner? Then, try to invent a moving practice for sending it.

GROUP PRACTICES - 15 minutes

1 Skipping rope each. Skip, running over the rope, one foot after the other. Can the whole group run, skipping, and share your third sensibly and safely? Leg movements are light but lively. Wrists gently do the turning of the rope.

2 Partners; with one large ball. Show me how you can send the ball a short distance to each other. I want neat, accurate and successful sending and receiving, please. Variety from a throw to be headed back; from a straight pass to a bounce return; or a kick, fielded and thrown back.

3 Hoops tag with three chasing seven. Dodgers are 'safe' when sheltering in a hoop. Unadventurous lingering in the hoop is discouraged by the teacher's 'Move!' Can you change your direction to avoid being caught? Chasers, remember to touch gently and safely.

Lesson Notes • 4 Lessons Development

WARM-UP AND FOOTWORK PRACTICES

1 The direction change is produced by stopping your forward movement with one foot pushing hard down into the ground, then pushing you off in the new direction. The knee of the braking leg bends, then stretches as it pushes you off again.

2 In all our chasing and dodging games we emphasise 'Touch gently to catch them. Hard pushing can cause a fall and a broken wrist or arm.' Emphasise also that we dodge away by sudden changes of footwork, including direction changes.

SKILLS PRACTICES: WITH A LARGE BALL

Individual practices

1 With slightly bent arms in front, throw up high enough for a catch with two hands at eye level. Restrain the long throwers.

2 Throw; bounce; catch needs judgement and planning to make the ball come up to just the right height for a catch at about waist level.

3 'Sending' has to be sufficiently gentle and restrained to keep the ball from disturbing others or leaving the play area.

Partner practices

1 Passing to one or other side of your partner gives them practice in 'Move early to be standing in position to catch.' This requires careful watching of the ball's height and speed.

2 Hands are spread at sides of ball, with thumbs back and fingers forward. Arms bend until ball touches chest, then the pass is made by stretching arms to push ball down to bounce just ahead of partner.

3 Class is asked to plan a simple practice to improve and develop the sending of a ball in their chosen way. The same way can be performed for the on-the-spot practice and for the running practice, or they can change the style of the second practice.

GROUP PRACTICES

1 Running over the rope, skipping, is easy physically, once the skill has been acquired. Because all are moving with ropes flying, they must share the space sensibly and not interrupt the movements of others. Main thoughts can be on the neat, small wrist action used to turn the rope, and on which foot is leading the action in going over the rope each time first.

2 In sending the large ball to a partner across a very short distance, we want an impression of neat, well controlled actions which can be successfully repeated. The receiving is as important as the sending. An interesting development would be for one partner to send it one way, and the partner to return it in a different way.

3 Hoops tag is played in one third of the area, using ten hoops as safe havens in which you cannot be caught by the chasers. Those caught take a coloured band and become another chaser.

Lesson Plan – 30 minutes

Emphasis on: (a) working almost non-stop to become and keep warm during winter; (b) practising to improve and remember simple skills.

WARM-UP AND FOOTWORK PRACTICES - 5 minutes

1 Can you show me some lively, warm-up activities, as you travel around the playground? (Look out for and encourage running, skipping, bouncing, hopping, jumping, slipping sideways, galloping.)

2 Dodge and mark with a partner. Marker runs after the dodging partner, trying to keep within touching distance. On 'Stop!' by teacher all must stop immediately to see who is winner – the dodger who can't be touched or the marker who is within touching distance.

SKILL PRACTICES: WITH A SKIPPING ROPE - 10 minutes

Individual practices

1 Put rope down, flat on the playground, well away from all others. Can you make a little pattern of jumps from one end to the other (e.g. jump and bounce over; jump and bounce back; stride, stride, stride, stride)? Balance on tiptoes back to the start.

2 Practise skipping freely. If you are just learning, practise stepping over the rope as it slides along the ground, slowly, towards you. Pull it well forward to hit the ground early.

Partner practices

1 Can you jump over the rope as it circles round, swung low by your partner? Change over after about four jumps.

2 Show your partner a favourite way to use the rope. If your partner skips, watch how he or she uses feet and legs (feet together or apart; one after the other; running; skipping; bouncing; straight or bent legs).

GROUP PRACTICES - 15 minutes

1 Large ball each. Practise dribbling by hand or foot. If I call 'Stop!' can you control your ball immediately? Use inside, outside and instep of foot for football dribble. Use fingertips for dribble by hand.

2 Skipping rope each. Can your whole group be aware of one another and try to show me a whole lot of different ways to use a skipping rope? Variety comes from rope on ground and in your hands; on the move and on the spot.

3 Partners; small ball each. Follow your leader who shows you some simple activities for the other to see and copy. To keep warm, try to keep moving for most of the time. You can throw and catch; dribble with foot or hand.

Lesson Notes • 4 Lessons Development

WARM-UP AND FOOTWORK PRACTICES

1 The opening activity uses the large leg muscles vigorously as the quickest way to produce body heat. Thereafter, by almost non-stop activity, it is hoped to keep them all warm. Standing, looking, listening, having long explanations, waiting for noisy children to behave, and anything else that inhibits action must be avoided or kept to a minimum.

2 Encourage dodgers to dodge with good direction changes or 'faking' to go one way, then going the opposite way, rather than dangerous, high speed running away from their pursuing partner.

SKILLS PRACTICES: WITH A SKIPPING ROPE

Individual practices

1 A 'pattern' implies more than one activity to practise the joining together with increasing control requirement in the NC. We want a well planned, joined up sequence of activities.

2 Most of the class should be skipping by now and able to keep very active and warm. Beginners will be trying to turn the rope overhead from wide hands to hit the ground in front to make the rope slide towards them to step over.

Partner practices

1 One partner swings the rope round in a big circle, low to the ground for the other to jump over. After three or four turns the one turning the rope must stop to avoid becoming dizzy, and change duties. We want a quiet, neat, high jump from two feet to two feet.

2 We are training their powers of observation and we hope that the observers will praise the work shown by their partners. They should be told to look first for the action and be able to give it a name. Then they look to see how the body parts are working and try to name the actions.

GROUP PRACTICES

1 Dribble by hand 'like a basketball player' or by foot 'like a footballer.' With both methods they are asked to keep the ball near enough to be able to stop immediately on the teacher's signal. When the teacher moves on to the next group activity, group members can take turns to call 'Stop!' and check the quick control.

2 The skipping group can be the one featured for a short demonstration, each time, before groups change round. We are looking for a group awareness of one another, sharing the space safely and sensibly, and trying to present a varied performance.

3 In follow the leader, using a small ball, two linked actions, possibly contrasting, would be most pleasing and welcome, particularly if performed in unison. Part of the contrast could be the accompanying actions of the feet, e.g. tiptoe walking balancing ball on hand; then jogging and basketball dribbling.

Lesson Plan – 30 minutes

Emphasis on: (a) performing simple, linked movements; (b) working vigorously to improve learning and to keep warm.

WARM-UP AND FOOTWORK PRACTICES - 5 minutes

1 Can you run and jump high over the lines? You can push off with one or both feet. Try to use your arms to help balance you, on landing.

2 Keep running and when I call a number, run quickly to join up with others to make a circle with that number in it. Three! (Repeat, calling 'Two!', 'Four!', and probably 'Three' again.)

SKILL PRACTICES: WITH SMALL BALLS - 10 minutes

Individual practices

1 Make lots of quick little throws and catches to a low height at about mid-chest. Catch with both hands well cupped and fingers pointing forwards.

2 Can you throw the ball up and a little way to one side of you, then run to catch it?

3 Walk forward, making the ball bounce up well from the ground, and catch it at about head height.

Partner practices

1 One throws to bounce ball to partner (about 3 metres apart), and then the other throws it straight back, without a bounce. Do four then change over.

2 Stand facing each other, about 3 metres apart. Throw up and to one side of your catching partner to make him or her move quickly to receive it.

3 Can you show me a way to send the ball to your partner, while keeping on the move (e.g. walking, side by side, throwing; bouncing in front for a catch; football passing)?

GROUP PRACTICES - 15 minutes

1 Free practice with a choice of ropes, hoops, bat and ball, large balls. Free practice of a lively activity to improve, and to be able to tell me how you have improved. Make it neat and be able to repeat it.

2 Small ball between two. Invent a game where one does something with the ball (e.g. counting bounces) while partner races round two markers, then change places.

3 Partners; bean bag or quoit. Play a lively one v one, throwing to make it land on ground on partner's side for a point. Decide how many points make a game, then change sides.

Lesson Notes • 4 Lessons Development

WARM-UP AND FOOTWORK PRACTICES

1 In running and jumping high over the lines, emphasise that they can run at an angle to a line, rather than always running straight at it, if that gives a better space to jump into. In an upward jump the leading leg is bent, with its knee and both arms reaching upwards, when you push off from one foot, as in athletics. We can jump up high from both feet as in jumping up to head a ball, or show different body shapes in flight.

2 Make a circle quickly is a fun game to practise a quick reaction and response to a signal. The teacher points to the quickest circles made.

SKILLS PRACTICES: WITH SMALL BALLS

Individual practices

1 Partners stand only 2 metres apart and try to throw almost non-stop, aiming at the partner's extended hands which show exactly where the ball is wanted for a quick in and out. 'The ball is hot. How many catches can you make in 30 seconds from . . . now!'

2 From a standing position, throw up to above head height and to 2 or 3 metres to one side of you. Run quickly to catch the ball, standing still, in a good position, with two hands. Watch the ball carefully at all times.

3 With a long arm, bounce the ball down and a little ahead of you to make it bounce up for a catch as you walk on to it.

Partner practices

1 The bounce throw to land a metre in front of your partner is thrown from shoulder height with one hand. The straight throw is made with a low, straight arm after a preparatory swing back. In both practices the catcher holds both hands forward to show where to aim.

2 The throw to above partner's head is aimed 2 metres to one side of your partner. This gives the catcher time to run in to position, place the hands correctly, and be still for the catch.

3 Talk about making the receiving easy by sending the ball in a considerate, 'sympathetic' way with as much care as possible.

GROUP PRACTICES

1 Whatever implement is chosen must be used for a lively activity to make and demonstrate an obvious improvement. An 'improvement' infers an impression of neatness, control, good use of space, confidence, and even polish and style.

2 Planning to invent a game or practice for two requires: a very limited, contained space; an identified activity; a method of scoring; and a main rule to keep the game going and fair.

3 'On partner's side' can simply be on the ground on partner's side of one of the paint lines, or preferably on partner's side of a long rope 'net' tied between chairs. Because it is one against one competitive, both must agree on how to serve, how to score and one main rule to keep the game enjoyable and fair.

Lesson Plan – 30 minutes

Emphasis on: (a) good dodging and chasing; (b) much demonstrating to and learning from a partner and others.

WARM-UP AND FOOTWORK PRACTICES - 5 minutes

1 Follow your leader, copying the actions being shown. Leaders, can you include some big and lively running and jumping actions, using arms and legs strongly?

2 Chain tag, with several pairs starting off as chasers. When the chains grow to fours with those caught joining on, they split to form two chasing pairs. Winner is last person to be caught.

SKILL PRACTICES: WITH HOOPS - 10 minutes

Individual practices

1 Put your hoop down on the ground well away from all others. Can you run round, showing me different ways to go into and out of all the hoops? (For example, in and land; in and straight out again; in and turn to face a new direction; one foot to same in to same out; in feet apart; in feet together.)

2 Carefully swing your hoop up in front of you with one hand to catch with two hands close together.

3 Walk beside your rolling hoop and show me how you use your hand to make it keep rolling beside you.

Partner practices

1 Try to show your partner how you can skip, using your hoop (e.g. low swings forward and back, side to side; on a diagonal; or with full swing overhead).

2 Can you bowl your hoop very slowly for your partner to bend and go through?

GROUP PRACTICES - 15 minutes

1 Large ball among four. In half of your area, play 2 against 2, and score by bouncing the ball in one of the two hoops in the opponents' half. Do not run with the ball. Pass to your partner with two hands for a two-handed catch.

2 Partners; each with a hoop. Show me some partner activity that you can invent with both working together and able to keep going (e.g.

mirroring, while skipping; rolling to each other, throwing up and catching). Hoop can also be on ground for balances.

3 Bat and small ball each. Practise freely, to 'feel' how gently the bat needs to strike the ball to make it bounce up or down. Use your wrist, not elbow or shoulder. Try balancing it for a few steps, then hit it up.

Lesson Notes • 4 Lessons Development

WARM-UP AND FOOTWORK PRACTICES

1 Follow your leader at a distance of 2 metres so that you can see the actions clearly and the ways that body parts are working (e.g. running with high knees raising and well bent arms followed by an upward jump from two feet to two feet with arms stretched sideways to help balance).

2 Start with four pairs as chasers. When caught you join on to the one who caught you. (If game is finished quickly by expert chasers, start with a different set of eight chasers.)

SKILLS PRACTICES: WITH HOOPS

Individual practices

1 Hoops are well spaced out on the ground to give an approach from all sides for a variety of ways into and out again. The variety will include different take-off and landing actions and uses of one, two or alternate feet. Body shapes in the air can vary and a change of direction can take place in the air or on landing.

2 Hoop is swung up with a long, smooth arm action to head height, gently released to carry on a short distance, then caught with both hands and brought down again.

Partner practices

1 If necessary, you can skip, using hoop on the ground, bouncing into and out, or circling around. A low swing with one hand from side to side is the next stage. Two hands can swing it low back and forward. Both hands can do the difficult swing overhead.

2 This activity needs a 30 or 36 inch (76-91 cm) hoop. One partner bowls the hoop slowly forward towards the partner who bends to come in from one side to step right through the hoop. An expert partner could try coming in from alternate sides, two or three times.

GROUP PRACTICES

1 Two little games are played in this group's third of the play area. For each game there are four hoops, placed in the corners. Explain to each couple which are 'their' hoops and which are the opponents'. A goal is scored by bouncing the ball in one of the opponents' hoops. The main rule is 'No running with the ball.' The groups can be asked to decide how to re-start after a goal. Groups can also be asked for a rule that helps to keep the game going and fair (e.g. defenders are passive while the ball is being passed, but they become active to stop a scoring attempt).

2 Partner activity in unison with hoops calls for thought and planning, and making allowances for a partner who might be less competent than you. We want something sufficiently simple to allow success and repetition.

3 Practise with bat and ball, on the move, and try continuous hits upwards; hits up to land and bounce up from the ground; and hits down using bat like a big hand.

Lesson Plan – 30 minutes

Emphasis on: (a) using a variety of implements in a variety of ways; (b) responding to many challenges.

WARM-UP AND FOOTWORK PRACTICES - 5 minutes

1 In your running, can you find your own nice, easy 'cruising' speed that you could keep going for a long time? Can you 'feel' your running rhythm? One, two, three, four; one, two, three, four.

2 All against all tag, counting how many times you are touched, and counting how many others you touch. Be gentle and careful with your touching/catching. No hard dangerous pushing.

SKILL PRACTICES: WITH A SMALL BAT AND BALL - 10 minutes

Individual practices

1 Bat your ball up and keep your best score. Use your wrist, not your elbow or your shoulder as you strike the ball. You do not need to hit it hard.

2 Walk forward, batting the ball down on to the ground, and keep your best score. Try to bring the ball up to about waist height.

3 Bat it up, let it bounce, bat it up. Strike it gently up and forward just far enough for you to meet it easily as you walk forward. As you bat it up, can you be very clever and hit it to a good space where you are not in someone's way?

Partner practices

1 One batting, one bowling gently underarm, can you hit the ball back for your bowling partner to catch? Stand about 3 metres apart only. After six practices, change places.

2 Both using bats, or one with bat and one using hand, play tennis over a line and see if you can keep going (rallying) for three or more which would be excellent. Stand only 3 metres apart.

GROUP PRACTICES - 15 minutes

1 Partners; with one small ball. Play hand tennis with or against your partner over a line 'net'. Can you make a rally of three or more which would be very good. Take your arm back ready each time, for a long swing.

2 Bat and small ball each. Practise using forehand, backhand strokes, and some striking up and down, on the spot and moving. 'Feel' now gently you can strike tor a good hit.

3 Follow the leader; choice of ropes, hoops large balls, bean bags. Try to link two or three ways of using your choice of equipment, and be able to repeat them (e.g. hoop-roll; throw up and catch; spin; or ball-throw and catch; dribble by hand; throw and catch).

Lesson Notes • 4 Lessons Development

WARM-UP AND FOOTWORK PRACTICES

1 Faster than jogging, slower than normal quick running, your 'cruising' speed feels easy. It has a steady, repeating, smooth rhythm.

2 In all against all tag, encourage the adventurous chasing after others as being as important as the dodging to avoid chasers. Often, pupils are only concerned with not being caught.

SKILLS PRACTICES: WITH A SMALL BAT AND BALL

Invididual practices

1 The ball is continually hit gently upwards from a quite high bat held near head and eye level where ball can be closely watched.

2 The hit downwards must be firm enough to bounce the ball up to about waist height for the next hit down. Because you are walking forward at the same time, the hit must be down and a little way forward.

3 In the batting up to allow it to bounce up for the next hit, you have to judge the amount of force needed, and judge the distance up and forward to hit it, to let you walk forward for the next hit.

Partner practices

1 Ball is bounced about 1 metre in front of the batter after a bowl high enough to bounce the ball up to waist height for the return hit. Batter should stand side-on to the bowler, hitting with bat face square to the catcher who holds hands forward as a guide and target for batter. By the sixth practice the batter should be feeling how much force is needed for a good hit.

2 In rallying to each other at only 3 metres to make it easy and controlled, the players must move quickly to stand side on to where the next return hit will be made. Bat is taken back each time in readiness for the hit.

GROUP PRACTICES

1 In co-operative, one with one hand tennis, each player stands 2 metres from the line 'net', and aims to land ball 1 metre in front of partner. This target area can be a chalk circle on each side. Players are asked to try to hit ball to partner's forehand side.

2 Forehand practice with palm uppermost and backhand hits with knuckles uppermost, can be practised by hitting ball straight up using each alternately. Forearm is turned in between.

This on the spot activity can be alternated with walking, hitting ball down to bounce up ahead of you to waist height.

3 Joining simple skills together, safely, 'with increasing control', is an expectation within the NC. This should influence their choice of implements for the follow the leader as they plan and practise linking ways to use them, and to be able to keep on repeating the sequence.

Lesson Plan – 30 minutes

Emphasis on: (a) enjoying the greater variety possible during warmer weather; (b) showing greater confidence and versatility.

WARM-UP AND FOOTWORK PRACTICES - 5 minutes

1 Run freely and quietly, listening for my shout of 'Change!' when you suddenly change direction. You do this by using one foot to stop you going the same way and to push you off on a new direction. Right foot would push you to the left, for example.

2 Dodge and mark with a partner. Use good footwork to dodge away from your marking partner. When I call 'Stop!' stop immediately to see who is winner – the dodger who can't be touched, or the marker who can still reach out to touch the dodger. (Change over and repeat.)

SKILL PRACTICES: WITH A SKIPPING ROPE - 10 minutes

Individual practices

1 Can you show me skipping on the move using a running action? Which foot is leading over the rope?

2 Can you skip with feet together using one bounce sometimes, and two bounces sometimes, between each turn of the rope? (Two bounce double beat for a nice, slow rhythm. One bounce for speed skipping.)

Partner practices

1 Ropes are placed parallel on the ground. With one hand joined, can you balance walk forward, backwards and sideways along the two ropes (slowly, feeling for rope, not looking down at it)?

2 Follow your leader at a safe and sensible 3 metres distance, trying to skip in unison using identical actions. Change places.

GROUP PRACTICES - 15 minutes

1 Quoit between two. Use a long rope, tied between chairs, as a 'net'. Can you win points by making the quoit land on your partner's side of the net? Decide how to serve to start each game. How many points in your game before you change sides?

2 Partners; with one skipping rope. Can you plan and show me a way that a couple can use one skipping rope? Rope can be on ground or held by one or both. One can swing rope low for other to jump over.

3 Large ball between two. Send your ball to your partner with two hands, then move to a space for the return pass. Pass; move; and receive, no more than 3 metres apart. Use two-handed chest pass. Move sideways into a space, to keep the 3 metres only gap.

Lesson Notes • 4 Lessons Development

WARM-UP AND FOOTWORK PRACTICES

1 On the teacher's 'Change!' one foot is firmly pressed down on the ground, stopping the forward movement. The knee of this braking leg is bent and then stretches, pushing you off in the new direction.

2 In dodge and mark with a partner, emphasise that sprinting away from the marker is not wanted. We want good dodging footwork, with changes of direction and speed as good examples. 'Stop!' means stop immediately, or the wrong person appears to be the winner.

SKILLS PRACTICES: WITH A SKIPPING ROPE

Individual practices

1 Running, or walking forward, stepping over the approaching rope as it slides slowly towards you, is an easy way to skip just after learning. The rope is being turned overhead with an easy wrist action.

2 'One bounce' and 'double bounce' mean the one or two beats of feet on ground between each swing of the rope. One bounce is the quicker, more physically demanding method. Two bounces should be encouraged for general use as it is much easier to keep going.

Partner practices

1 Hands joined, friendly balancing along parallel ropes has many possible combinations. Both can face the same direction, forward, sideways or backwards. Each can face a different way. The non-balancing leg and foot can be lifted, stretched and held up in a variety of interesting ways.

2 The 3 metres gap is to prevent the follower's rope going over the head of the leader and causing an accident. A simple running over the rope action with the same leg leading, together, is a spectacular example of partner work.

GROUP PRACTICES

1 Play competitive, 1 against 1, quoits, if they are sufficiently skilled in aiming and catching. If not, they should play co-operatively to develop those skills. 'Net' rope should be at about chest height. Aim with one hand and catch with both.

2 Inventing a way for two to use one skipping rope with good control and success should inspire a great variety of ideas. By putting the rope group on show each time we can extend the class repertoire which also extends the teacher's repertoire.

3 The sending and the receiving are equally important elements to be aware of and practise. A third element of equal importance is the 'move to a new space' after each sending of the ball. By moving to one side and forward, the players will always be only 2 to 3 metres apart, a distance at which all the practising can be good.

Lesson Plan – 30 minutes

Emphasis on: (a) linking movements together smoothly; (b) co-operating with a partner in a variety of ways.

WARM-UP AND FOOTWORK PRACTICES - 5 minutes

1 Can you show me the difference between running and jumping long and running and jumping high, over the lines on the playground (straight leading leg with foot leading in long jump; bent leading leg, knee leading in high jump)?

2 Free and caught. Six chasers try to 'catch' others by touching them gently on arms. When caught, stand still with hands on head. Those not caught can free those caught by touching them on the arm. (Change chasing group often.)

SKILL PRACTICES: WITH A SMALL BALL - 10 minutes

Individual practices

1 Can you bat the ball upwards a little distance with a flat hand? What is your best score? Five is very good.

2 Now use your hand to bat the ball downwards on to the ground. Can you walk about, batting ball down just ahead of you?

3 Can you hold the ball ready in one hand, bat it straight up with the other hand, then catch it with both hands?

Partner practices

1 Bat the ball to your partner with a flat hand. Partner catches it and bats it back to you. The ball is batted from being held ready in the non-batting hand.

2 Stand about 3 to 4 metres apart, with a line or a mark between you to aim at. Try the overhead throw from just above your shoulder, and count your own good hits.

GROUP PRACTICES - 15 minutes

1 Medium ball among four. Hoop 'chase and hide' with two chasing team players trying to touch two dodgers with ball. Six hoops, well spaced out on ground are 'safe' hiding places where dodgers can't be caught. When both dodgers are caught, teams change duties.

2 Small ball between two. Aiming and catching at numbered spaces marked with chalk. Try a long, overarm aiming action, with ball starting above shoulder.

3 Partners; small bat and ball. Can you invent a simple practice or game that uses bowling and batting? For example, in a small corner, bowl to partner who gently bats it away, and runs to touch corner, etc., and back, for a point before bowler touches mark. (N.B. Limit the area to a very small space to give fielder a chance.)

Lesson Notes • 4 Lessons Development

WARM-UP AND FOOTWORK PRACTICES

1 Demonstrate with good performers to show what you mean by 'straight leading leg with foot well forward' in the lively long jump, and the different, more springy, upward, high jump 'with the leading leg bent'.

2 As in all chasing and catching/touching games, emphasise that the chasers must be gentle in their catching with no hard, dangerous pushing, which could knock someone over and break an arm or a wrist. Encourage good dodging, and trying hard to release some of those caught.

SKILLS PRACTICES: WITH A SMALL BALL

Individual practices

1 Batting the ball up with a slightly cupped hand is a good preparation for using a bat. Emphasise the gentle, little wrist action with almost no movement in elbow or shoulder. Good footwork is needed to take you to where the ball bounces.

2 Batting down on to the ground and just ahead of you lets you practise 'on the move'. Aim to hit ball hard enough to bounce it up to about waist height.

3 Ball is held in non-striking hand above the hitting hand. Hit is made by bringing striking hand up against the ball to hit it straight up for an easy one-handed catch. Timing of release is the difficult part.

Partner practices

1 At about 2 metres apart, the strike can be gentle and the catch, with both hands, is not too testing. Go for only one hit for a catch rather than the very difficult non-stop rallying to each other, which they will otherwise try with many mis-hits.

2 This aiming at a line practice can be tried with a high, overarm action, starting with the ball above the shoulder of the throwing hand. Catcher stands with both cupped hands reaching well forward, ready to react to receive the ball. Make it competitive, with one against one, or our pair against the rest.

GROUP PRACTICES

1 'Hoop chase and hide' is played in half of the third in which the group is playing in and around their six hoops. The two chasers may not run, carrying the ball. They must pass to each other to pursue the dodgers they are trying to touch with the ball.

2 Partners stand 4 metres apart. Once again, they use the overarm action to aim at the numbered spaces to score 1, 2 or 3 points. The competition can be partner against partner, or pair of partners trying to outscore all the other couples.

3 Mini-rounders or cricket, or whatever they agree, must be limited to a tiny part of their area with agreement on the main rule, how to score, how to be 'out' and when to change places.

Equipment: 30 small balls; three medium size balls; five small bats.

Lesson Plan – 30 minutes

Emphasis on: (a) demonstrating increasing control over body and implements; (b) demonstrating the ability and desire to plan, practise, repeat and improve.

WARM-UP AND FOOTWORK PRACTICES - 5 minutes

1 Follow your leader who will demonstrate a lively sequence of a short walk, a short run and a jump. Watch your partner's feet carefully and see if the two of you can build up to moving in the same way, in unison. (Variety from small or large movements, bent or stretched legs and arms, one or both feet take-off and landing.)

2 Six cross court sprints. Partners stand side by side down middle of court. On signal 'Go!' both race to touch own side line with one foot and race back to touch partner's hand. (After six times teacher nominates 'First . . . second. . . third . . .)

SKILL PRACTICES: WITH A SMALL BAT AND BALL - 10 minutes

Individual practices

1 Can you bat the ball upwards softly to about head height, using your wrist and not your elbow or shoulder as the moving part?

2 Can you repeat this, walking forward, and try to catch the ball, balanced still, on the bat, every so often? From this balance, start hitting it up again.

3 Can you bat the ball upwards from being held ready in the non-batting hand, let it bounce once, bat it up, then catch it and start again?

Partner practices

1 Batter, strike the ball gently for partner (2 metres away, only) to catch with both hands. Have six goes and change duties.

2 Can you stand side by side, both batting upwards gently? When you have agreed your best team score before one stops, change to both batting down on to ground, again counting your best score.

GROUP PRACTICES - 15 minutes

1 Skipping rope each. As a group, can you plan to show off many ways to use a rope, including skipping, working alone or with a partner? (Skipping on the spot and moving; feet together and apart, etc.)

2 One small bat and ball among three. Can you invent a simple little game that uses bowling and batting in a very small space? (2 against 1 batter who must run, when ball is hit, to score runs. Fielders get batter 'out' in agreed ways.)

3 Partners; one quoit. Rope 'net' tied between chairs. 1 against 1 quoits, trying to make it land on opponent's side for a point. Throw with one hand, catch with two, and aim to deceive your partner by aiming left and right.

Lesson Notes • 4 Lessons Development

WARM-UP AND FOOTWORK PRACTICES

1 'Sequence' means a group of linked actions, smoothly joined to one another. A short walk of about four steps; a short run of about four strides leading into the jump which can bring the whole sequence to a still finish, with a two-footed landing, or the jump be on to one foot which starts the next group of walking steps, without stopping.

2 Insist that they touch side line, or better still, put their foot down just over the line. If they jump into their turn and land in a crouch 'sprint start' position, facing back towards their partners, the race will be speeded up. About six sprints spread the race out sufficiently to see the winning order which should be called out, as far as possible.

SKILLS PRACTICES: WITH A SMALL BAT AND BALL

Individual practices

1 'Feel' how much effort to put into the hit as you send ball up to about head height only. Hold bat at mid-chest height where you can see ball well. A gentle wrist action is all you need.

2 Walk; hit up several times; catch ball still on bat by going up to meet it coming down, and letting bat 'give' to stop ball bouncing. Hold the balance, then start all over again.

3 Ball is hit upwards from hand as in a table tennis serve. It bounces up, is batted up again, and is then caught with one hand.

Partner practices

1 The batter's short, gentle strike to partner's outstretched and cupped hands, is made from a hit from the hand (as in **3** left), or after dropping the ball to bounce straight up and then hit.

2 Non-stop, co-operative batting: (a) straight up and down between partner and you, is followed by (b) hitting the ball straight down to bounce up between you. One bounce between hits is the target and a 'best score' of six or more deserves encouraging comment, with a demonstration.

GROUP PRACTICES

1 The group, as a whole, is trying to present a set of varied skipping activities. Such a presentation informs the teacher and the class of the repertoire possible with this implement which can be used in games lessons all year round.

2 The bowl, bat, hit, run, field and try to get out simple game must be played in a very limited area, with the batter never allowed to hit the ball hard out of the area. The group needs to agree one main rule for the batter; how 'out'; and how to change round.

3 It is helpful to have chalk lines down the side of each little 'court', separating it from the ones beside it. Because the game is competitive, the players need to agree on where to serve from; how to score; and how many points to play for in each game.

Equipment: 30 small bats and balls; ten skipping ropes, five quoits.

Lesson Plan – 30 minutes

Emphasis on re-establishing tradition of: (a) immediate responses to instructions; (b) enthusiastic and vigorous participation; (c) safe and sensible sharing of space.

WARM-UP AND FOOTWORK PRACTICES - 5 minutes

1 Show me that you can run quietly, without following anyone. Lift heels, knees, arms and head, and run straight, not curving. (Unless taught otherwise, children run in an anti-clockwise circle.)

2 Can you use this best, straight running to visit every part of our playground 'classroom' within the four outer lines? Visit the ends, sides, corners and the middle sometimes.

3 When I call 'Stop!', show me how quickly you can respond and stand, balanced on tiptoes, on the nearest line, arms stretched sideways to help your balance.

SKILL PRACTICES: WITH SMALL BATS AND BALLS - 10 minutes

Individual practices

1 Walk about with ball balanced on bat, near eye level. Now change to gentle batting upwards using wrist action only. What is your best, new year score? Five or more is very good.

2 Throw ball straight up with one hand, let it bounce up, bat it up, catch it with one hand. Repeat.

3 Can you walk about, looking for good spaces always, batting your ball down on to the ground?

Partner practices

1 Can you and your partner keep your ball up in the air between you, using gentle strokes by using your wrists only? (Not elbows or shoulders, which are far too powerful for this neat stroke.)

2 Can you strike the ball up to land between you for a return strike by your partner? Stand only two or three steps apart and keep your best score.

3 One bowls underarm with a very slow and low lob for partner to bat back to bowler for catching practice. Have six goes and change.

GROUP PRACTICES - 15 minutes

1 Large ball between two. Practise ways to send the ball to your partner, both standing and on the move. How many body parts can send ball quite accurately?

2 Fours; one bat and ball; half the area. Can you make up a simple batting game, using bat, ball, skittles and lines to 'contain' games? How will

you score? How will you be 'out'? How many balls each?

3 Skipping rope each. Free practice to revise and try out some of the many ways of skipping. On the spot, feet apart or together, or one after the other. Moving in different directions.

Lesson Notes • 4 Lessons Development

WARM-UP AND FOOTWORK PRACTICES

1 Class needs a start of year reminder of what 'good running' means or they will return to the noisy, anti-clockwise running in one big circle, typical of much primary school running.

2 Running along straight lines, not curves, enables you to visit every part of the teaching space because you are continually coming to an outside line and needing to change direction. Such 'non following' in physical education practising gives each child lots of room and time to perform, unimpeded.

3 Exercises in listening and responding immediately to the teacher's signals and instructions are important. Poor responders can be made to behave and respond better so that valuable time is not wasted waiting each time for someone.

SKILLS PRACTICES: WITH SMALL BATS AND BALLS

Individual practices

1 'Performing simple skills safely to join them together with increasing control' satisfies a main requirement within the NC. Balancing, alternate with a little hit upwards, watching the ball closely and using just the right amount of force, is a difficult skill for young pupils.

2 Batting the ball almost straight upwards to let it bounce almost straight upwards for the next hit, needs a gentle touch, using a wrist action, not elbow or shoulder.

3 Using the bat like a big hand they now hit the ball down and a little way forward as they walk forward, trying to make the bounce up come nicely to where the next step will take them.

Partner practices

1 Standing next to each other, each in turn bats the ball straight up between them. The other partner makes the next little hit up. They have to be told to stand 'close enough to touch your partner' so that a vertical (and very gentle) hit is possible.

2 Still close together, they hit the ball gently and straight up, high enough to make it bounce up for the partner to hit up.

3 At 3 metres apart the bowler aims a 'low and slow' lob to land about 1 metre ahead of the batter to bounce up for a hit at chest height, ideally side-on to the bowler and catcher.

GROUP PRACTICES

1 A variety of ways to send (including throwing), receive and travel with a ball is a NC emphasis. The ways they receive and control are as important as the sending.

2 In half of their third of the teaching area, they are challenged to 'invent a simple batting game'. They must agree on the style of the game, how to score, how to involve all in the game fairly, and the one main rule that keeps the game going and fair.

3 Free practice will be as varied and challenging as a teacher commentary and praise can make it. Quiet, neat footwork; good rope control; and varied directions and speeds are encouraged.

Lesson Plan – 30 minutes

Emphasis on: (a) practising, almost non-stop, to improve; (b) practising good footwork, including dodging and chasing; (c) practising varied ball skills.

WARM-UP AND FOOTWORK PRACTICES - 5 minutes

1 Run, practising little side steps to avoid others coming towards you. In a side step one foot goes out to the side instead of forward, to put you on to a new line, still facing the same way.

2 Five points tag. All have five points to start with. When touched you lose one of your points. (N.B. No dangerous pushing. Touch gently.)

SKILL PRACTICES: WITH A LARGE OR MEDIUM BALL - 10 minutes

Individual practices

1 Walk, throwing the ball just above your head, and catching. Keep your fingers spread, thumbs back fingers round the sides.

2 Bounce the ball using your finger-tips, left and right hands, on the spot, and weaving in and out of the others.

3 Dribble the ball like a footballer, keeping it close. When I call 'Stop!' see how quickly you can control the ball by placing a foot on top of the ball, to make it still.

Partner practices

1 About 3 metres apart only, throw a two-handed pass to your partner and move sideways into a space for the return pass, still only 3 metres apart. Pass; move; receive.

2 Shadow dribbling, one ball. Leader shows partner favourite ways to dribble, using feet or hands. After six touches, change over and see if the follower can copy the routine exactly.

GROUP PRACTICES - 15 minutes

1 Quoits; with a partner; 1 v 1. Long rope 'net' tied between chairs. Play quoits and try to score by landing quoit on a partner's side for a point. Decide how to start, how many points to a game, and any other rules to help the game.

2 Large ball among four; 3 v 1. 'Wandering ball' with three of group on outside of big chalk circle passing the ball across the circle, bypassing and outwitting the one in the circle. Keep changing one in centre who works hard to intercept the ball.

3 Partners; with a hoop each. Stand at opposite side of court from partner. Bowl hoop to pass each other and go to partner's line. Keep close to and in control of your hoop. Now can you show me another good partner practice you like?

Lesson Notes • 4 Lessons Development

WARM-UP AND FOOTWORK PRACTICES

1 To give continuous practice of meeting others, the side step is done in one third of the teaching space, to bring everyone close together. The running is at half speed to let them focus on and do the side steps in safety.

2 In five points tag, the class is asked to dodge away from chasers, not race away at high speed.

'Dodging' means changing direction; side stepping; and making sudden changes of speed, including stopping suddenly. The game is stopped every 16 seconds to let the teacher check on 'Who were the best dodgers with 5 points still? Who were the best chasers, catching 3 or more?'

SKILLS PRACTICES: WITH A LARGE OR MEDIUM BALL

Individual practices

1 The throw to above the head is performed from a high position at head height with the ball in both hands, arms slightly bent, and fingers pointing upwards. Hands receive with a little 'give' each time, and eyes watch the ball closely.

2 In bouncing, basketball fashion, we use the fingertips and a wrist action, up and down where you stand, and forward and down when travelling. Use left and right hands to avoid others coming towards you.

Partner practices

1 The two-handed chest pass starts in front of the passer's chest with hands higher than elbows. Ball is pushed to partner's chest height for a catch where the arms 'give' to stop ball rebounding away. The move sideways to a new space to receive the next pass is one of the most important moves in invasion games. 'Pass, then move!' will continually be said during games lessons from now on. This movement is needed by a team to advance itself and the ball towards the opponents' goal line.

2 Shadow dribbling trains the leader to think about and plan a short sequence, and trains the follower to observe and be able to repeat the sequence.

GROUP PRACTICES

1 In competitive, 1 against 1 quoits, the 'net' is a long rope tied between chairs or higher objects, ideally at chest height so that the throw has to be high enough to 'let the quoit see over the net'. A point is scored if the quoit lands on the ground. Pairs have to agree how to start or serve; ways to score; and one main rule designed to keep the game going and fair.

2 In 'wandering ball' or piggy in the middle

round a chalk circle of 2 metres diameter, the 3 must stay outside the circle, and the 1 must stay inside it. If the game keeps breaking down with few passes being made, the 1 can be asked to be passive, keeping arms by the sides, to make passing easier.

3 Bowling the hoops to change places, line to line, is done at a walking pace, keeping beside your hoop, not pushing it far ahead.

Lesson Plan – 30 minutes

Emphasis on: (a) linking movements with increasing control to keep the action going longer; (b) making up and playing simple games.

WARM-UP AND FOOTWORK PRACTICES - 5 minutes

1 Change between easy jogging and bursts of sprinting. Jog when you are near others. Sprint when you see a good space. Arms and heels are low in jogging, lifted up when sprinting.

2 Chain tag with four couples starting off as chasers. When someone is caught, he or she joins the pair that caught them. When the chain grows to four, it separates into two chains of one couple each who then continue to chase. Winner is last one caught.

SKILL PRACTICES: WITH A SKIPPING ROPE - 10 minutes

Individual practices

1 Practise the slow overhead pull and the easy step over as the rope slides along the ground towards you. Hand action is very small.

2 Now skip on the move with a sort of running action. Which is your leading leg?

Partner practices

Stand where you can see each other easily. A will skip for about six travelling counts and stop. B will skip for about six counts and stop. Can you include a variety of directions and try to have one of the pair on the move at all times? Your working-resting partner skipping will be interesting if you can do some opposites (e.g. forwards, backwards; feet apart, together).

GROUP PRACTICES - 15 minutes

1 Large ball among four; 2 v 2. Play 2 against 2 in half of your area, and score by bouncing ball in one of the choice of hoops. Can you agree one main rule to help keep game fair? What other way to score can you think of to give more goals?

2 Long skipping rope among four. Two swing rope low, for others to come in to. While learning, do not swing the long rope overhead.

Come in to the rope when it is swinging away from you. Leave the rope left when it is swinging to the right.

3 Bean bag among three; 2 v 1. Piggy in the middle with the two with the bean bag moving to a space to receive from partner. Middle person tries to intercept by spreading arms and legs wide. Use two-handed pass, then move to a new space, ready.

Lesson Notes • 4 Lessons Development

WARM-UP AND FOOTWORK PRACTICES

1 The teacher can demonstrate easy jogging with arms and heels lower than normal lively running, an upright body, and with a nice, steady rhythm. Short bursts of sprinting for 4 to 6 metres through a space has rapid short strides, a high lift of heels and knees, and a body inclined forward.

2 In the chasing and dodging chain tag, chasers must touch gently and safely, and not push the dodgers to catch them. Encourage the dodgers to try side steps, direction changes and sudden changes of speed to evade chasers, never high speed running away.

SKILLS PRACTICES: WITH A SKIPPING ROPE

Individual practices

1 All practise the slow, overhead pull to remind themselves of the easy, wide hand action and the physically easy step over the rope.

2 The slow step over the rope becomes a quicker run over it as the class try to skip 'on the move', noting which leg is leading. This one foot after the other is easier, physically, than skipping on the spot with feet together. 'Easier' means you can keep going and keep warm as we move into colder weather.

Partner practices

Resting and working; watching and doing; alternate skipping gives them a rest and challenges them to plan a sequence that has variety (and quality, we hope) of actions, leg shapes, directions and speeds. 'Someone working at all times' means a smooth transition from one performer to the partner, with excellent timing.

GROUP PRACTICES

1 The competitive, 2 versus 2, with one ball in half of their third, requires the passing pair to 'Pass, then move to a new space to receive the next pass' or they will never advance themselves or the ball, because you may not run carrying the ball. To make this feature succeed, it might be necessary to ask the two defenders to be passive, never going for the ball when it is being passed, but able to intercept shots.

2 A long rope of 4 metres long is swung low, from side to side, vigorously. (Not overhead to start with.) Group has turns at swinging the rope, then trying to come in to skip. They should aim to come in to skip along the line on the ground where the rope touches each time. Beginners usually jump too early at a point where the rope is well off the ground.

3 The pair with the bean bag are asked to wait until the receiving partner has moved sideways into a space before throwing to that partner. They must not throw it over the head of the one in the middle. If this game is being badly done with few successful passes and catches, ask the one in the middle to be passive and not challenging for the bean bag.

Lesson Plan – 30 minutes

Emphasis on: (a) near-continuous, lively action to become and to stay warm; (b) strong leg activity which increases winter warmth.

WARM-UP AND FOOTWORK PRACTICES - 5 minutes

1 Follow the leader, where the leader uses a simple repeating pattern, e.g. walk 6, jog 6, jump with feet together for 6. Change over and see if follower can remember and repeat it all.

2 'Line safe tag', where the six chasers can catch you if you are not on a line, i.e. on a line is safe, untouchable. Those caught take a coloured band and become chasers. If dodgers are staying too long on their lines, teacher calls 'All move!'

SKILL PRACTICES: WITH A BEAN BAG - 10 minutes

Individual practices

1 Jog forward, throwing up and forward a little way with one hand, and catching with two hands.

2 Throw low (chest height), throw medium (head height), throw high (as high as can be caught reliably), and try to do this on the move to keep warm.

3 Stand. Throw bean bag to one side or the other; in front of you; or behind you. Can you move quickly to catch it with two hands? Throw it high enough to give you time to get there.

Partner practices

1 Jog round, side by side, passing the bag like a rugby ball with long straight arms swinging across from side to side. Throw and catch with two hands. Aim just in front of your partner.

2 Stand 3 metres apart. Throw with one hand, move to a new space and catch with two hands. Hold your hands forward to show your partner a target to aim at. Pass; move; receive, moving sideways and forward to maintain the 2–3 metres distance.

3 Stand very close. Throw above partner's head for a high jump up to catch at full stretch with one or both hands.

GROUP PRACTICES - 15 minutes

1 Free practice; with choice of ropes, hoops, balls, quoits, bats and balls. Choose something you can use in a lively, vigorous way, using large body actions, as you share the space sensibly.

2 Bean bag among four; team passing; 2 against 2, or 3 against 1. (2 v 2, if good skill level; 3 v 1 if not so good.) Keep close enough to give partner an easy 2–3 metres pass. Three good passes can equal a goal.

3 Partners with a large ball. Keep on the move to show me how you can carry, send and receive your ball with lots of success, keeping going, almost non-stop, to keep warm.

Lesson Notes • 4 Lessons Development

WARM-UP AND FOOTWORK PRACTICES

1 To inspire an instant response the class can be asked to follow the leader doing the teacher's suggested, simple, short sequence with its walk, jog and jump, always looking for good spaces to lead your partner through. When 'pattern' is understood the class can be invited to keep the same simple sequence or adapt it to one of their own planning. Each part must be kept short.

2 Because December can be very cold we do not want too many instances of inactive loitering on the 'safe' lines. After 20 seconds, the teacher checks on who were the best dodgers, still not caught, and changes the chasers over.

SKILLS PRACTICES: WITH A BEAN BAG

Individual practices

1 Because it is easy to catch and hold, a bean bag is a good implement for cold weather throwing and catching, as it does not roll or bounce away from you. The little throw forward is to about head height and just ahead of you.

2 Still jogging while practising to keep warm, still throwing with one hand and catching with two, they feel the different amounts of force needed to make it go 'Low; medium; higher'.

3 A standing throw up and to one side or to the front is followed by a quick move to a position where you can catch the bean bag while standing still with hands forward and cupped – another example of 'simple skills joined together.'

Partner practices

1 In jogging side by side, emphasise that your body is facing forward normally with long, low arms swinging from side to side, with the hands round the sides of the ball. (Children often run with their whole body moving sideways, not facing to the front.)

2 This 'Pass, then move!' practice is one of the most important in games. The move, usually to one side and forwards, into a space, means that you are available to receive the next pass in a space, and the ball is advancing towards the opponents' line.

3 Jumping partner must wait until ball starts to come down before he or she jumps up to meet it at full stretch, then land, nicely balanced, with feet astride.

GROUP PRACTICES

1 In free practice in December, the main feature must be the vigorous action asked for, to keep warm. Ideally, whole body actions, able to be repeated, non-stop, are being planned and practised, e.g. running style skipping with high knee raising.

2 Competitive 2 v 2, or 3 v 1, team passing with a bean bag, gives excellent practice in the important 'Pass, then move for the next pass – in a space you have made by moving.'

3 The three part sequence asks for a controlled carry, a sending that is accurate and neat, and a receiving that looks easy because the receiver is in the right place and ready.

Lesson Plan – 30 minutes

Emphasis on: (a) engaging vigorously in activities to keep warm; (b) co-operating with a partner to improve and extend skills.

WARM-UP AND FOOTWORK PRACTICES - 5 minutes

1 Follow your leader who will show you two or three lively actions to warm up the big muscles, particularly the legs. Can you copy these actions precisely? (Look out for, comment on and encourage jogging, sprinting, jumping, bouncing, hopping, skipping, leaping.)

2 Couples tag. Four couples start off as chasers. When one of the pair touches a dodger, the caught boy or girl changes place with the one who caught them to form a new chasing couple.

SKILL PRACTICES: WITH A LARGE BALL - 10 minutes

Individual practices

1 Carry ball in both hands like a rugby player. Run about and when I call 'Change!' place your ball down like a rugby player scoring a try, and pick up a different ball. Continue running and listening for my signal to 'Change!'

2 Throw ball up and forward a short distance ahead of you. Run to catch with two hands near eye level.

Partner practices

1 Jog, side by side, passing the ball, rugby fashion, a short distance in front of your partner to let him or her run and meet it each time. Use two hands and a lot of care.

2 Make two-handed chest and bounce passes to each other at about 3 metres apart. After every pass, move sideways and forwards to a new space to receive the return pass. Pass; move; receive.

GROUP PRACTICES - 15 minutes

1 Skipping rope each. On the spot, practise the slow double beat of feet for every turn of the rope, and the quicker single beat. Skip on the move and show me your best style of non-stop skipping. Direction changes are interesting.

2 Five large balls among group of ten. Five with balls are dodging away from the others who are trying to touch a ball to gain it. Rugby style game with ball carriers allowed to run, carrying in both hands. Touch ball gently, not the person.

3 Large ball among four; 2 v 2; half pitch. Invent a 'three lives' game with one pair having three attacks to score. After defence steal ball three times, teams change duties. Decide how to score; one main rule to keep game going; and how to re-start after a goal.

Lesson Notes • 4 Lessons Development

WARM-UP AND FOOTWORK PRACTICES

1 In mid-winter the class can be told about this first, energetic activity, while still in the classroom. Partners can be arranged and the action can start immediately they reach the play area. Stoppages for explanations or demonstrations will be kept to a minimum, and most of the teaching and praising takes place while the class is moving.

2 Couples tag keeps them moving vigorously in pursuit or dodging. It also keeps them thinking as the catcher breaks away from the pair and the newly caught joins on. The game is stopped every 30 seconds or so to check on 'Who are the good dodgers, not caught at all?' and to introduce new chasers.

SKILLS PRACTICES: WITH A LARGE BALL

Individual practices

1 Ball is carried in both hands with straight arms hanging low in front of you. With the rhythm of the running the ball is gently swung from side to side. On 'Change!' ensure that the ball is placed, not dropped, with downward hands pressure, on to ground.

2 Throw up and forward a short distance. Make throw high enough to allow a catch near eye level with two hands. Be sensible about the space you throw in to. Avoid others.

Partner practices

1 Emphasise low carry of ball in front of you. Arms swing from side to side naturally. Keep body facing forward while running, but twist upper body to face partner as you pass ball just ahead of him or her, high enough for a good mid-chest catch.

2 Chest pass is aimed at partner's chest. Bounce pass is aimed at ground about 1 metre in front of partner. After every pass, move to a new space, but still only about 3 metres apart. If 'Pass, then move! Give, then go! Pass, run to a space!' is emphasised at this age, the quality of team play, now and in the junior school, will be greatly improved.

GROUP PRACTICES

1 Give them something to think about, and plan while skipping on the spot or moving. Single and double beat foot action on the spot for slower or quicker skipping, with one or two bounces for each rope turn. On the move can be with feet together, or like running with one foot after the other.

2 Rugby ball touch is helped by your being allowed to run, holding the ball in rugby. Teacher can add interest by calling 'Change!' when all the carriers must put the ball on the ground and let the other half of the group become the dodgers.

3 Three lives' games played in one direction only have the same attackers and defenders until the defenders steal possession thrice. This allows two little games to be played in the one third. Teams need to decide the one main rule, the scoring method, and how to re-start after a score.

Lesson Plan – 30 minutes

Emphasis on: (a) showing increasing control over own movement; (b) linking movements to demonstrate increasing versatility

WARM-UP AND FOOTWORK PRACTICES - 5 minutes

1 Can you run and jump high, run and jump long over the lines and show me the difference? (High, at medium speed, rocking up on take-off foot, with leading bent knee reaching up. Long, at speed, with long, straight, leading leg well forward.)

2 Teacher's space tag. Teacher and four helpers 'guard' the middle third of the playground, touching the remainder to prevent them scoring a point for a clear run to opposite side of third. Four helpers are changed over often.

SKILL PRACTICES: WITH A SKIPPING ROPE - 10 minutes

Individual practices

1 Choose one way to skip that you find easy. Can you all keep going for a whole minute, starting from . . . now!

2 Can you link together a way of skipping on the spot with one on the move, and keep alternating them?

Partner practices

1 Place ropes on ground, side by side, about 1 metre apart. Can you make up a little balancing sequence along the ropes as a pair? (For example, one or both hands joined, balancing sideways, forwards or backwards; or facing in different directions.)

2 Watch your partner doing a favourite piece of skipping. Tell your partner what you liked about it. Change.

GROUP PRACTICES - 15 minutes

1 Large ball between two. Can you invent a 1 against 1, simple game, using one ball and part of a line? How will you score? What is main rule to keep game going? How will you re-start after a score? (For example, 1 v 1, to hand or foot dribble to cross line.)

2 Partners with rope each. Play follow the leader, where the leader, 3 metres ahead, demonstrates at least two actions for a partner to copy. Watch your leader's feet, together or apart; and actions, walking, running, bouncing; and the directions.

3 Hoop 'safe' tag with eight hoops. Three chasers wearing bands chase to touch the remainder, when they are not 'safe', in a hoop. Those who are caught take a band and become extra chasers. If dodgers 'hide' too long in hoops, teacher calls 'All move!' Gentle touches by chasers. No hard, dangerous pushing.

Lesson Notes • 4 Lessons Development

WARM-UP AND FOOTWORK PRACTICES

1 For unimpeded, safe, continuous practice, they should be reminded to 'visit every part of the playground space, never following anyone' and not run in an anti-clockwise circle, typical of much primary school running, all following one another.

2 Because dodgers are running towards one another across the middle third, they must do so with great care to avoid head-on bumps. Dodgers should be using clever footwork such as direction changes and side steps, and not racing flat out.

SKILLS PRACTICES: WITH A SKIPPING ROPE

Individual practices

1 Easy skipping includes the slow overhead pull and the step over the rope sliding along the ground towards you; running action skipping with one foot leading over the rope; skipping on the spot, slowly, with a double beat of the feet for every swing over of the rope. (Jump and bounce.)

2 Progression in physical education includes moving on from simple and isolated movements to making short sequences of linked movements. Here we want skipping on the spot linked to skipping on the move.

Partner practices

1 The words 'balancing sequence' which is the challenge here, mean that more than one way to balance must be planned and practised. One could be with hands joined, one without a join; facing same way could alternate with facing opposite ways.

2 Watching and commenting on a partner demonstration trains them in observing the elements of movement. What actions? What use of body parts? What directions? What speed? Saying something about it trains them in reflecting and evaluating which are important requirements within the NC.

GROUP PRACTICES

1 In a specified, limited area they are challenged to 'Invent a competitive, 1 against 1 game.' They have to plan, decide and agree on the nature of the game; how you score within it; what is the one main rule; and how to restart after a goal or point has been scored.

2 The follow the leader skipping sequence must have at least two parts to be a sequence, featuring linked actions. Apart from quality, of course, a good sequence includes variety and contrast, e.g. feet together, going sideways quickly, then running feet going forwards slowly.

3 In hoop 'safe' tag, coloured bands are placed on the ground for the newly caught to pick up and wear, as they join the other chasers. Particularly if the weather is cold, the dodgers should be told to 'Linger seldom. Move often' to keep warm and give chasers some activity in pursuing.

Lesson Plan – 30 minutes

Emphasis on: (a) varied activities possible with a hoop; (b) demonstrating enthusiastically when asked and watching others' demonstrations with interest and helpful comments.

WARM-UP AND FOOTWORK PRACTICES - 5 minutes

1 Run quietly, following no-one. When I call 'Change!' change direction by pushing hard with one foot to stop your forward movement and to make you go another way. Right foot firmly pressed on to ground pushes you off to the left, to run facing a new direction.

2 All against all tag, trying not to be caught by others. No hard, dangerous pushing. Touch gently. (Teacher checks best number caught by chasers, and least times caught by dodgers.) A sudden direction change is a good dodge.

SKILL PRACTICES: WITH HOOPS - 10 minutes

Individual practices

1 Place all hoops on ground, well spaced out. Run and jump over some hoops and quickly step in and out of some hoops. Pretend some are obstacles and some are stepping stones. When I call 'Stop!' show me how quickly you can find a hoop to stand in. (Repeat.)

2 Can you walk forward, either bowling your hoop, or doing low, two-handed little throws and catches? Share the space sensibly and don't bump or throw towards others.

3 There are many ways to skip using a hoop, including skipping round it, while on the ground; plus using one or two hands, forward and back, side to side, or diagonally; swinging low; or overhead like a skipping rope. Show me what you can do.

GROUP PRACTICES - 15 minutes

1 Partners, with a quoit. 1 against 1, to make the quoit go over the long rope 'net' tied between chairs or netball posts. Decide how to start and score; one main rule to keep game going; and how many points in a game.

2 Hoop each. Try spinning the hoop on the ground, ankle, wrist or waist. Jog beside your hoop, bowling gently with one hand across top of hoop. Can you spin the hoop to make it come back to you?

3 Larger ball among four; 2 v 2; end line touch. Play in half of your area with several ways agreed to score, e.g. touch end line; bounce in one of hoops in the corners; pass to partner on end line. Decide a main rule to keep game going, and how you re-start.

Lesson Notes • 4 Lessons Development

WARM-UP AND FOOTWORK PRACTICES

1 Pupils have been changing directions in every games lesson, but probably without thinking about the technique involved. Here we are consciously stopping the forward movement by pressing down hard on one foot which also then sends us off with a strong push into the new direction. A lean of the upper body into the new line is helpful.

2 In all against all tag, encourage practice of sudden direction changes to evade a chaser following or coming towards you. For safety's sake, insist on 'Gentle touching only so that no-one is knocked down and hurt.'

SKILLS PRACTICES: WITH HOOPS

Individual practices

1 All 30 hoops being used in the lesson are well spaced out, with ten in each third. Some are placed just close enough to act as 'stepping stones'. A rhythmic pattern is possible. 'Jump over; jump over; step and step and step.'

2 In bowling, walk beside your hoop with your fingers across it, pointing away from you, just below the top. Pull with your hand to try to roll it forward. In throwing and catching, with both hands wrapped round the hoop, close together, the hands open and close, keeping some contact throughout.

3 Skipping with a slow, short, one-handed swing from side to side, is like skipping over a low rope swinging from side to side, and is the easiest to start with, before progressing on to two-handed swings overhead. Two bounces of the feet to each rope swing are recommended.

GROUP PRACTICES

1 In competitive, 1 against 1 quoits, you score if the quoit lands on the ground on your opponent's side of the rope 'net' which is at head height. One hand is used for throwing and two are used for catching. Some chalk marks for the side of each little 'court' are recommended, to contain the game.

2 Free practice with a hoop allows more time to practise the skills performed or seen earlier in the lesson and to try out some of the teacher's challenges. 'Can you . . . ?'

3 Played in half of a third of the teaching space, 2 v 2 with a large ball aims to encourage each pair to keep possession and to try to advance themselves and the ball to score in ways that they agree. More ways to score make the defending pair space apart more to cover, for example, the end line and the two hoops. Spreading the defenders gives the attackers more room and more chances to score. In this game and quoits we hope that the players will decide: how to score, often using more than one way; how to re-start after a score; the one main rule that helps to keep the game going.

Lesson Plan – 30 minutes

Emphasis on: (a) showing good planning in safe, appropriate solutions to tasks; demonstrating good control over body, good sharing of space, and good footwork to be in the right place at the right time.

WARM-UP AND FOOTWORK PRACTICES - 5 minutes

1 Can you mix quick walking, easy jogging and short bursts of sprinting as you use the whole playground carefully and safely? In jogging, heels and arms are carried low. In your sprints, lift heels and knees strongly.

2 Count how many two-footed jumps you need to cross from one side line to the opposite side line. Use your arms strongly to pull you far forward. Swing them forward, then back with a bend of the knees, then swing them forward and spring from both feet.

SKILL PRACTICES: WITH SHORT TENNIS RACKETS AND BALL - 10 minutes

Individual practices

1 Can you bounce the ball continuously up from your racket? Use a gentle wrist action with racket held near eye level.

2 Can you bounce your ball continuously down on to the ground? Try this standing, then slowly moving forward, still using the wrist action only. No hard hitting with elbow or shoulder.

3 Throw ball up straight to let it bounce up. Hit it up, let it bounce, catch it with non-hitting hand and start again. What is your best score of controlled hitting and catching?

Partner practices

1 Throw ball to partner who strikes it back for an easy catch. Hit it gently and change over after five catches.

2 Both with a racket now, can you very gently keep the ball bouncing once only, between hits, as you hit low and slow to each other? Start by dropping the ball, letting it bounce up, then sending it. Stand about 4–5 metres apart only, and be gentle.

GROUP PRACTICES - 15 minutes

1 Ten hoops on ground. Invent a chasing and dodging game, using the hoops and keeping inside your own area. Chasers wear bands. Decide the main rule, how caught, what to do when caught.

2 Short tennis racket each. Practise by yourself to improve your ball and racket control. You can practise on the spot, hitting up, down or a mixture. Moving, you can hit up, down and from side to side.

3 Large ball among four. Team passing with 3 against 1. The 3 try to keep the ball and make passes. 1 tries to 'steal' the ball by vigorous chasing after the ball. 1 can be passive if passing is not good, and needs help.

Lesson Notes • 4 Lessons Development

WARM-UP AND FOOTWORK PRACTICES

1 'Easy' jogging is done with an upright body, small steps, arms and heels carried low, and is easier than quick walking. The sprinting strides are rapid, with hands and heels carried higher, and are tiring and space consuming, so done in short bursts through spaces where others are not impeded.

2 A series of standing, two-footed jumps is performed with each jump starting at the place where the previous one landed. Feet apart with toes turned in slightly; a long arm swing forward, back with a knee bend, and forward strongly with the dynamic stretch of the legs; and a low layout in flight, all help the jump to be as long as possible.

SKILLS PRACTICES: WITH SHORT TENNIS RACKETS AND BALL

Individual practices

1 Racket is held near its face, not near the end of its handle, to give a better control, and it is held near the chest so that the ball can be watched closely.

2 Because the racket is springy it does not need to apply much force in batting the ball down to bounce up to waist height for the next hit down. We want them to 'feel' how much or how little force is needed. Beginners hit too hard usually.

3 Throwing up; letting bounce; hitting straight up; and catching are another example of 'performing simple skills and joining them together with increasing control', as required within the NC.

Partner practices

1 If ball is bounced about 1 metre in front of batter and comes up to just above waist height, the batter has an easy return to the bowler whose hands should be cupped and forward, ready.

2 In hitting very gently to each other they should again aim to bounce the ball 1 metre in front of partner to give him or her the best possible chance to return it. 'Low and slow' to land for an easy return, ideally from partner's forehand, is the aim.

GROUP PRACTICES

1 With ten inventing and playing a chasing and dodging game, the teacher might initially suggest three chasers wearing bands who can catch you if you are not in a hoop, 'safe' and untouchable. This will give the game a start from which other suggestions will follow from the pupils, e.g. when caught, take a band and become a chaser; 'hiding' in the hoop to be no more than 5 seconds.

2 Racket skills are the most difficult and seldom practised away from school. Personal practice aims to reinforce the work done earlier in the lesson with individual coaching by the teacher.

3 Team passing, 3 against 1, is a most important practice for our traditional invasion/running games, such as netball, football, hockey and basketball, to encourage running to a space to be available for a return pass, well away from opponents.

Lesson Plan – 30 minutes

Emphasis on: (a) running, jumping, throwing and skipping; (b) practising to improve performance; (c) dependence on a partner to provide the unpredictable situations so often found in games.

WARM-UP AND FOOTWORK PRACTICES - 5 minutes

1 Follow your leader who will show you some actions as you run and jump. For example, hurdling, scissors jumping, long and high jumps, and two-footed take-off long jumps.

2 Side line sprints. Couples stand side by side down the centre of the area. On the signal 'Go!' each sprints to the nearer side line, touches it with a foot and races back to touch partner's hand. A signal 'Four!' or 'Six!', for example, will start a race where they sprint to the line and touch it, four or six times.

SKILL PRACTICES: WITH A SMALL BALL - 10 minutes

Individual practices

1 Throw up and catch with two hands at eye level. Now do the same thing, walking and keeping an eye on the ball.

2 Walk forward, throwing ball up to bounce in front of you. Catch it after the bounce.

3 Can you walk, batting the ball down on to the ground with left and right hands?

Partner practices

1 One partner throws straight for other to catch. Second partner bounces it back. Change over after six.

2 Roll ball for partner to ground field, pick up and roll back.

3 Stand on opposite sides of a line, about 3 metres from the line. Throw, aiming to hit the line and give partner a catch.

GROUP PRACTICES - 15 minutes

1 Partners; skittle and a small ball. Bowl to bounce up to hit skittle. Partner is wicket keeper who throws or rolls ball back. Have six goes each and change over, keeping your own best score. Can you work out where a 'good length bounce' would land?

2 Partners; skipping rope each. Can you show me some examples of what we might call 'partner skipping'? You can use own rope and follow the leader, or watch each other's favourite practice. You can try to skip together, using one rope only.

3 Hand tennis over line or rope 'net'. Serve by dropping ball, letting it bounce up, and then striking it to land on partner's side of net. Decide the one main rule to keep the game fair and going. How many points in a game before changing ends?

Lesson Notes • 4 Lessons Development

WARM-UP AND FOOTWORK PRACTICES

1 May is an appropriate month for using athletics terminology and explaining and showing, for example, hurdling, scissors jumping, as well as long and high jumping. In hurdling over lines approached from the front, we swing up and down with a straight leading leg and a trailing leg that lifts out and to the side, then forward. A scissors jump from an angle swings the nearer leg up and over the line.

2 In side line sprints, everyone starts on the signal. They must touch their own side line and their own partner. Cheating must be looked out for and strongly objected to, so that the true winners are the winners.

SKILLS PRACTICES: WITH A SMALL BALL

Individual practices

1 Class can all stand, throwing and catching with two hands at eye level, so that teacher can check hand positions and height thrown. If this is satisfactory, they practise on the move, with well cupped hands and eyes looking closely at the ball.

2 A throw up and forward, with a swing back and forward with a long arm, aims to go just high enough and far enough forward for the next bounce to come up nicely ahead of you for a catch.

3 Continuous batting downwards, 'as in basketball', is usually well done by this age group, and is easier with a hand than with a bat or racket. A gentle wrist action is all that is needed.

Partner practices

1 At a distance apart of 3 metres, one throws straight to the partner's outstretched hands in front of chest with a long underarm aiming action. The other partner throws a bounce return with ball starting high above the shoulder, and aiming to land it 1 metre in front of partner, for a chest height catch.

2 Still 3 metres apart, they roll ball for partner to crouch to field with both hands behind the ball, with fingers facing down.

3 Aiming to hit a line between you and your partner is done with a high starting position with ball above shoulder.

GROUP PRACTICES

1 Bowler aims underarm to land in front of wicket skittle to bounce up to hit it. The many which miss this difficult target will be fielded by the wicket keeper who rolls ball back to the bowler.

2 Year 2 partner skipping produces a most interesting variety of work, as the pupils approach the end of their year. The work deserves to be demonstrated as a way of expanding the class repertoire, and the teacher's repertoire. Skipping together, using one rope only, is now achievable by some.

3 For this competitive, 1 against 1, hand tennis game over a long rope 'net', they need to agree on: how to serve; how to score; and any allowances to make to keep the game going and fair.

Lesson Plan – 30 minutes

Emphasis on: (a) variety from individual, partner and group activities; (b) variety from running, skipping, throwing and striking a ball; (c) variety from planning, doing, reflecting and commenting.

WARM-UP AND FOOTWORK PRACTICES - 5 minutes

1 With a partner, run side by side at the same speed. Each has a turn at setting the rhythm of the running. Run in good style, with good lifting of heels and knees, and with whole body 'straight ahead'.

2 Jumping alternately, see how few standing long jumps your partner and you need to take you from side line to opposite side line. One jumps and stands still in landing place. Two starts behind toe line of one and does his or her standing, two-footed long jump. Count how many (or few) jumps you needed. Try to improve on the way back by really driving hard and long into your strong leap.

SKILL PRACTICES: WITH A SKIPPING ROPE - 10 minutes

Individual practices

1 Can you link together two or three ways of skipping including one on the spot and one on the move?

2 Choose one way you enjoy skipping and find easy to keep going. Let me see if the whole class can be brilliant and keep going for a minute. Ready? ... Begin!

Partner practices

1 With ropes placed parallel on the ground, can you make up a little balancing sequence along the ropes, as a pair (e.g. side by side or facing each other; one or both hands joined; balance walk forward, sideways or backwards)?

2 Can you remind each other of some examples of the 'partner skipping' you tried last month? Practise again and try to do something, using one rope only.

GROUP PRACTICES - 15 minutes

1 Groups of four; short tennis racket or small bat and ball. Two with two tennis over a long rope 'net' tied between chairs. Co-operate to keep a long rally going and keep your best score without a stoppage.

2 Skipping rope each. Can your whole group practise to show the class a group demonstration of varied skipping – ones, pairs, on the spot and moving, fast and slow, feet together and apart?

3 Large ball among four; in half of area. Can you invent a game for four players, using one ball and the lines round your area? How will you score? What will be your main rule to keep the game fair and going?

Lesson Notes • 4 Lessons Development

WARM-UP AND FOOTWORK PRACTICES

1 Partners running at the same 'cruising' speed should 'feel' the repeating rhythm that is being quietly sounded out by their feet. It should be slow enough to allow a good lifting of knees, heels, arms and head. Keep together, one, two, three, four!

2 In a standing (start) broad jump, start with feet slightly apart with toes turned in a little way. Swing both arms forward high, back with a good knees bend, and forward hard as you do your reach into your long jump. Pull both feet forward to land.

SKILLS PRACTICES: WITH A SKIPPING ROPE

Individual practices

1 Skipping on the spot and on the move mixes the more demanding actions on the spot with the physically easier ones, while on the move. We can challenge them, 'Can you skip with feet together then moving one after the other?', or 'Can you turn the rope to the front while you travel backwards?', or 'Can you include one quick jump for each turn, then the slower two jumps for each turn of the rope?'.

2 Skipping inspires leg muscle action which inspires heart and lungs action, leading to improved fitness. Many primary school children express an interest in becoming fitter and they can test themselves by trying to keep going for a minute's skipping, which is something they can then practise at home.

Partner practices

1 Ask them to try some of the many ways that a pair can join for balancing with a support. As well as both facing the same way, they can have one going forwards, one going backwards. Tell them to 'Feel for the rope with each foot before putting your weight down. Feel for it. Do not look down for it.'

2 Partner skipping can include: following the leader; one watching, the other copying; a mirroring sequence that changes after an agreed number of repetitions; or the difficult pair skipping with only one rope, held by one or both.

GROUP PRACTICES

1 Co-operative tennis over a low rope 'net' to 'Find your best score as a group. Can you keep going for six good hits? Ask them to move early to be in position for the return hit, ideally in a 'side-on' position. Start by dropping the ball for a good bounce up to hit.

2 Emphasise that each rope group will give a demonstration to show variety, quality, and excellent, shared use of space, and to increase the class skipping repertoire. Look out for and comment on: on the spot and moving; different directions and speeds; solo and duo; varied actions in feet and legs.

3 With one large ball among four, the eventual game invented will probably have 2 v 2, or 1 v 3; will be played in half of the group's area; and will need one main rule and a scoring system.

Lesson Plan – 30 minutes

Emphasis on: (a) planning and performing safely a range of simple actions and linked movements in response to given tasks; (b) demonstrating improvements, generally, in performances that are accurate, consistent and look 'easy'; (c) reflecting competently in pointing out key features and expressing pleasure, after observing a performance.

WARM-UP AND FOOTWORK PRACTICES - 5 minutes

1 Jog easily, 'coasting' along at a speed which you think you can maintain almost as easily as quick walking. In your jogging, arms and heels are lower than in stylish or fast running. Can you 'feel' this rhythm which you find easy to continue?

2 Cross court relays. Partners stand, side by side, down the middle of the area. On 'Go!' one partner sprints to touch his or her nearer side line, then sprints back to touch partner's outstretched hand. Second partner sprints to own, nearer side line, then back to touch first partner's hand. This continues until the pair have made the number of touches asked for, when the teacher tries to call out the results.

SKILL PRACTICES: WITH A SMALL BALL AND BAT - 5 minutes

Partner practices

1 Batting partner, strike the ball from one hand, high, to give partner an easy catch. Catcher, roll the ball back to your partner. Have six goes and change.

2 Batting partner, strike ball along ground to give partner fielding practice. Fielder, send ball back to batter with one bounce for an easy one-handed catch. Have six goes and change.

3 French cricket. Bowler aims ball to hit partner on the leg below knee height, from about 2 metres, slowly and gently. Batter guards legs with bat held low and turns ball away. Fielder next throws from where he or she picked up the ball. (Game is kept contained by insisting on gentle aiming and hitting.) Change when bowler hits legs of batter.

GROUP PRACTICES - 20 minutes

1 Long rope in groups of four. Two take turns at swinging the rope low from side to side. Skippers try to come in, skip several times, then move away from the still swinging rope.

2 4 v 4; three catch rounders. Batting team has one innings each, striking ball to land in the limited area being used. Batters all follow hitter round the diamond of three skittles. Fielders make three catches and shout 'Stop!'. Batters score one run for each skittle.

3 Partners; short tennis; 1 v 1. A competitive game played over a line or rope 'net'. Decide how to serve to start game, and how to score. How many points in a game before changing ends?

Lesson Notes • 4 Lessons Development

WARM-UP AND FOOTWORK PRACTICES

1 Easy jogging has lower arms and heels than normal athletic, good style running. The steps are shorter and there is a feeling of a continuing rhythm which the runner should be able to feel 'Jog; jog; easy; easy. One, two, three, four. One, two, three four.'

2 In cross court relays, emphasise that they touch just over the line, each time, with a foot.

Also, they must wait to be touched by the incoming partner. (The over-competitive touch short of the line, and go before being touched.) A crouched, sprint start position by the second runner gets him or her off to a more explosive start.

SKILLS PRACTICES: WITH A SMALL BALL AND BAT

Partner practices

1 Ball is struck from hand as in a table tennis service. Striker should be side-on to receiving partner. 3 metres apart is an easy distance and sufficient for receiver to see ball's speed and flight, and react. 'Keep your best team score of good hits and catches out of 12.'

2 Batter tries to send the ball along ground, without bouncing, for partner to field with both hands and body behind ball. Hands are wide spread with fingers down towards ground, and small fingers can be crossed to 'make a floor for the basket made by the hands'.

3 In French cricket, make it a main rule that the ball stays in the limited area the pair is using. In other words, 'No big hits!' Bowler is encouraged to bowl underarm at a good length, to land ball about half a metre in front of the batter's legs, which are the target. Batter plays a purely defensive stroke to push the ball away 2 or 3 metres to what is the next bowling position.

GROUP PRACTICES

1 In long rope skipping in fours where two swing and two skip, the rope swingers only swing the rope from side to side, if the skippers are learners. With more expert performers the rope is swung in a complete circle. Both learners and experts move in to skip as the rope swings away from them (i.e. in from left as rope swings up to right). They leave rope one way as it swings the other (i.e. out to left as rope moves to right).

2 In 4 against 4 rounders, the main rule is that the ball must not leave the area allocated. When each one of batting team has had one hit, the teams change over. The three catches of the fielding team must involve three different players. Bowler is asked to bowl underarm to let ball bounce about 1 metre in front of the batter. A bat or a hand can be used for the striking to enable easy hitting.

3 The competitive 1 against 1, short tennis, over a long, low rope 'net', can be better contained if chalk marks are made at the sides of each little 'court'. The easiest serve is to drop the ball to make it bounce straight up to be hit at about mid-chest height. Encourage them to stand 'side-on' to their opponents, with the chest facing to one side, not towards the opponent.

Index